P9-DEE-074

Grilling
MAESTROS ②

FUNDING PROVIDED BY:

 weber®

CENTENNIAL CELEBRATION
100 YEARS BV
SINCE 1900
BEAULIEU VINEYARD
1900-2000

Cuisinart
SAVOR THE GOOD LIFE™

RECIPES FROM THE PUBLIC TELEVISION SERIES

Produced by Marjorie Poore Productions

Grilling 2
MAESTROS

With Marcel Desaulniers
Chris Schlesinger, and Fritz Sonnenschmidt, C.M.C.

Photographs by Alec Fatalevich

Table of Contents

Introduction

This is the second volume of recipes from the public television series *Grilling Maestros* featuring chefs Marcel Desaulniers, Chris Schlesinger, and Fritz Sonnenschmidt, C.M.C. Those of you who have watched the programs are aware of the exciting and innovative recipes that these three master grillers present week after week, all of which are contained in this book.

A little more than fifty years ago, cooking outdoors had become almost as extinct as the people who first made fire. Technology provided everything needed to cook indoors in a perfectly controlled environment. But something was missing. Technology could not replace the seductive aromas of outdoor cooking, the excitement and challenge of working with live fire, or those special, bold flavors that multiply exponentially in foods cooked on a grill.

Yet, despite their love of outdoor cooking, people still get stuck in what we call the "steak–burger–chicken" rut, making the same things over and over. That's where our maestros come to the rescue. Their mission is to give people wonderful recipes and ideas to make their grilling adventures much more interesting and enjoyable. As some of the most creative cooks in the industry, they have each developed a wonderful assortment of recipes that truly get the juices flowing.

Marcel Desaulniers comes from the world-famous Trellis Restaurant, which turned Williamsburg, Virginia, into a culinary as well as historic destination. The Trellis Restaurant and Chef Desaulniers established a reputation in the 1980s as one of the first to use only menus consisting of fresh, in-season ingredients. He also took the throne as the "king of chocolate" with his land-mark "Death by Chocolate" desserts and cookbooks. Grilling has always been an important part of the Trellis Restaurant repertoire, and we are indeed fortunate that Chef Desaulniers has so generously shared his grilling secrets, in the form of easy-to-make and elegant recipes, with us.

BV

1/3 MILE TO

BEAULIEU VINEYARD

WINERY OPEN TO VISITORS 10-5

LEFT SIDE ON HWY 29

Maestro Chris Schlesinger did for grilling in the 1980s what Julia Child did for French cooking in the 1970s. Many of us grew up on grilled hamburgers, hot dogs, and an occasional steak or chicken—usually burned beyond taste recognition. We might still be eating those barbecue staples if it weren't for Chris, chef/owner of the popular East Coast Grill in Cambridge and the Back Eddy restaurant in Westport, Massachusetts, where the food is as sensational as the setting. His books *Thrill of the Grill* and *License to Grill* opened our eyes to the enormous variety of foods that are at home on the grill and taught us how to combine those ingredients with flair. His lessons also help grillers understand fire, which can be their best friend or worst enemy. Just watching Chris will give any hesitant cook enough confidence to approach a grill with passion.

Maestro Fritz Sonnenschmidt, C.M.C., has a heart warm enough to light any grill and big enough to take any culinary student—whatever their level—under his tutelage. As the culinary dean of the prestigious Culinary Institute of America, he is one of those gifted teachers and masters who attract students from all over the world. His expertise extends into every area of cooking, but those who know him well are aware of his special passion for grilling. His demonstrations clarify some of the essentials of grilling, such as control of heat, flavor pairing, and doneness. His recipes—along with a generous portion of his humor—make everything come out right.

We hope you enjoy this second collection of recipes from these three grilling maestros. Their generosity in sharing their expertise and recipes allows us all to enjoy the infinite pleasures of outdoor cooking.

—*Marjorie Poore, Producer*

Beginnings and Endings

Grilled Asparagus and Sautéed Wild Mushrooms on Toasted Brioche

Marcel Desaulniers

Brioche

1 tablespoon granulated sugar

¼ cup hot water

Pinch of saffron (about 1 gram)

1 tablespoon dry active yeast

2 cups all-purpose flour, sifted

1 teaspoon salt

2 large eggs, beaten

6 tablespoons plus 1 teaspoon unsalted butter, softened

Mushroom Cream

2 tablespoons unsalted butter, cut into 4 pieces

¼ cup minced yellow onion

Salt and white pepper to taste

¼ cup dry white wine

¾ ounce dried wild mushrooms

2 cups heavy cream

Asparagus

1 tablespoon extra virgin olive oil

1 pound asparagus, ends trimmed, peeled, blanched in boiling salted water, and shocked in ice water

Salt and white pepper to taste

4 tablespoons unsalted butter, cut into 8 pieces

1½ ounces wood ear mushrooms, sliced into ⅛-inch-thick strips

1 ounce black trumpet mushrooms, picked clean of twigs, and sliced into ¼-inch-thick strips

continued on next page

This makes a delicious and attractive luncheon dish, especially when you use an interesting and tasty assortment of wild mushrooms. If you are short on time, purchase the brioche from a high-quality bakery.

SERVES 4

Grilled Asparagus and Sautéed Wild Mushrooms on Toasted Brioche (continued)

Asparagus (continued)

1½ ounces chanterelle mushrooms, picked clean of twigs, and sliced ⅛ inch thick

1½ ounces shiitake mushrooms, stems removed, and caps sliced ⅛ inch thick

5 fresh plum tomatoes, washed, quartered, and slow roasted in the oven

1 tablespoon chopped fresh herbs

IN THE BOWL of an electric mixer fitted with a dough hook, dissolve the sugar in the hot water. Add the saffron and set aside for 10 minutes to steep. Add the yeast and stir gently to dissolve. Allow the mixture to foam for 2 to 3 minutes.

ADD THE SIFTED FLOUR, salt, and eggs to the yeast mixture. Combine on low speed for 1 minute. Scrape down the sides of the bowl, then continue to mix on low speed until the dough forms a ball, about 2 minutes. Scrape down the sides of the bowl, and pull the dough off the hook. Adjust the mixer speed to medium–low and begin to add the 6 tablespoons of butter, 2 tablespoons at a time, being certain the butter is thoroughly incorporated before adding the next 2 tablespoons. (When most of the dough attaches itself to the dough hook, stop the mixer and pull the dough off the hook.)

COAT THE INSIDES of four 8–ounce soup crocks with the remaining 1 teaspoon of butter and set aside. Remove the dough from the mixer and form it into a smooth ball. Place the dough in a stainless steel bowl, cover with a dry towel, place in a warm location, and allow to rise until the dough has doubled in volume, about 1 hour (depending on the warmth of the space). Punch down the dough to its original size and cut it into 4 equal pieces. Shape into balls and place each in a prepared soup crock, cover with a dry towel, place in a warm location, and allow to rise a second time until the dough has doubled in volume, about 1 hour (depending on the warmth of the space).

PREHEAT THE OVEN to 350°F. Bake the brioche for 25 to 28 minutes, until the surface is golden brown. Cool the baked brioche in the crocks for 15 minutes. Remove the brioche from the crocks and cool to room temperature before slicing ¼ inch off the top of each bread. Use a soup spoon to remove the center portion of brioche, leaving a cavity in the center.

TO MAKE THE MUSHROOM CREAM, heat the butter in a medium saucepan over medium-high heat. Add the yellow onion, season with salt and white pepper, and sauté until tender, about 1½ minutes. Add the white wine and stir to combine. Add the dried mushrooms and stir to combine. Cook the mushroom mixture for 3 minutes until almost dry. Add the heavy cream and stir to combine. Bring to a boil. Reduce the heat and simmer until thick, about 5 minutes. Remove the mushroom cream from the heat, strain through a medium-mesh strainer, and keep warm. Chop and reserve the cooked mushrooms and onions for the presentation.

FOR THE ASPARAGUS, drizzle the olive oil over the blanched spears. Season with salt and white pepper. Grill the asparagus over a medium-hot fire, turning frequently until they become nicely browned. Remove from the grill and keep warm.

REDUCE THE GRILL HEAT to low and toast the brioche, cut side down, on the grill until warm and golden brown in the cavity. Keep warm.

IN A SKILLET, heat the butter over medium-high heat. Add the wood ear, trumpet, chanterelle, and shiitake mushrooms. Season with salt and white pepper and sauté until half cooked, about 4 minutes. Add the reserved chopped mushrooms and 4 tablespoons of the mushroom cream and stir to incorporate. Reduce the heat and simmer slowly for 2 minutes. Remove from the heat and keep warm until needed.

EVENLY DIVIDE THE REMAINING mushroom cream among 4 plates. Place a brioche in the center of the sauce. Evenly divide and artfully arrange the asparagus in the brioche cavity. Then fill the cavity with the warm sautéed mushrooms. Garnish the plate with the roasted tomatoes and a sprinkling of fresh herbs. Serve immediately. ◉

Grilled Shrimp and Bacon Skewers with Pickled Onion and Avocado Salad

Chris Schlesinger | Reprinted from *License to Grill*, William Morrow and Company

1 red onion, peeled, halved, and thinly sliced

1 cup white vinegar

2 avocados, peeled, pitted, and diced

¼ cup fresh lime juice (from about 2 limes)

¼ cup extra virgin olive oil

1 tomato, cored and diced

1 tablespoon ground cumin

1 teaspoon minced garlic

¼ cup roughly chopped cilantro or parsley

Salt and freshly cracked black pepper to taste

1 pound medium shrimp (16 to 20), peeled and deveined, tails left on

½ pound slab bacon, cut into 16 equal cubes, blanched in boiling water for 1 minute, and drained

½ red bell pepper, cored, seeded, and cut into 8 pieces

4 scallions, white and green parts cut into pieces about 1 inch long (about 16 pieces)

2 tablespoons vegetable oil

IN A SMALL BOWL, combine the onion and vinegar and let stand for 1 hour. While the onions are pickling, combine the avocados, lime juice, olive oil, tomato, cumin, garlic, cilantro, salt, and pepper in a medium bowl. Toss well, cover, and refrigerate.

AFTER THE ONIONS have soaked for an hour, drain them and discard the vinegar. Add the onions to the avocado mixture.

THREAD THE SHRIMP, bacon, bell pepper, and scallions alternately onto skewers. Sprinkle the skewers with the vegetable oil, salt, and pepper and grill over medium heat for 3 to 4 minutes per side. To check for doneness, cut into one of the shrimp to be sure it is opaque throughout.

REMOVE THE SKEWERS from the grill. Place the salad on a serving platter or individual plates, top with the skewers, and serve. ◉

Red onions, a mild variety, are soaked in vinegar to take away their bitterness and rawness. Be sure to watch the bacon on the grill since the fat can cause flare-ups.

SERVES 4

Grilled and Chilled Mediterranean-Style Gazpacho

Chris Schlesinger | Reprinted from *License to Grill*, William Morrow and Company

The grilled vegetables give this gazpacho a wonderful boost of flavor. Watch the eggplant carefully to make sure it is thoroughly cooked, but still moist all the way through.

SERVES 4

1 large eggplant, cut into rounds about 1 inch thick

3 fennel bulbs, trimmed, cored, and sliced

2 red bell peppers, halved and seeded

1 red onion, peeled and cut into rings about 1 inch thick

¼ cup olive oil

Salt and freshly cracked black pepper to taste

1 quart tomato or Clamato juice

2 cups chicken stock

1 tablespoon minced garlic

¼ cup fresh lemon juice (from about 1 lemon)

½ cup red wine vinegar

2 tablespoons ground cumin

2 tablespoons ground coriander

¼ cup roughly chopped fresh parsley

¼ cup roughly chopped fresh basil

About ½ cup freshly grated Parmesan cheese (optional)

IN A MEDIUM BOWL, combine the eggplant, fennel, bell peppers, and onion with the olive oil, salt, and pepper. Toss to coat the vegetables with the oil. Place the vegetables on the grill over medium-high heat. Grill the fennel and onion until tender and slightly charred, 3 to 4 minutes per side. Grill the eggplant and bell peppers until browned, 4 to 5 minutes per side. As the vegetables are done, remove them from the grill and cut them into small chunks.

IN A LARGE BOWL, combine the grilled vegetables with all the remaining ingredients except the cheese and mix well. Cover and refrigerate until well chilled. Serve sprinkled with Parmesan. ◉

Grilled Sesame Chicken Skewers

Chris Schlesinger | Reprinted from *License to Grill*, William Morrow and Company

¼ cup coriander seeds

2 tablespoons white or black peppercorns

¼ cup sesame seeds

⅓ cup soy sauce

2 tablespoons fresh lime juice (from about 1 lime)

1 tablespoon brown sugar

1 tablespoon Tabasco sauce or other hot sauce

2 pounds boneless, skinless chicken breasts, cut into about 20 large chunks

4 scallions, white and green parts finely chopped

2 tablespoons minced ginger

2 tablespoons sesame oil

2 red bell peppers, cored, seeded, and quartered

2 red onions, peeled and quartered

Salt and coarsely ground black pepper to taste

2 limes, quartered, for garnish

IN A SMALL SAUCEPAN, combine the coriander, peppercorns, and sesame seeds and toast over medium heat, shaking the pan, until the first wisp of smoke appears, 2 to 3 minutes. Remove from the heat and allow to cool. Place the cooled spices on a flat surface with a small sauté pan on top of them. Holding the handle with one hand, place the other hand, palm side down, in the center of the pan and apply pressure, rolling the pan over the spices to crack them.

IN A SMALL BOWL, combine the soy sauce, lime juice, brown sugar, and Tabasco. Mix well and set aside.

IN A MEDIUM BOWL, combine the chicken chunks, scallions, ginger, and sesame oil and toss well. Thread the chicken onto 4 skewers alternately with the bell pepper and onion chunks. Sprinkle with salt and pepper and grill over medium heat for 5 to 7 minutes per side. To check for doneness, cut into the chicken to be sure it is opaque all the way through.

PLACE THE CHICKEN SKEWERS on a platter and sprinkle with the spice mixture. Garnish with the lime wedges and serve the soy dipping sauce on the side. ◉

Grilled meat and seafood skewers are sometimes called *yakitori*, which means grilled in Japanese. The method of toasting and then cracking spices brings out tremendous flavors in them.

SERVES 4

CHICKEN WINGS FOUR WAYS

Chicken Wings Teriyaki

Fritz Sonnenschmidt

½ *cup soy sauce*

¼ *cup rice wine*

1 teaspoon grated orange zest

1 teaspoon grated fresh ginger

1 clove garlic, smashed

1 teaspoon grated lemon zest

¼ *cup peanut oil*

2 pounds chicken wings (about 10 whole wings)

2 stalks celery, cut into sticks

Soy Sauce Dip

⅓ *cup soy sauce*

⅓ *cup balsamic vinegar*

½ *teaspoon powdered green tea*

1 tablespoon brown sugar

1 teaspoon finely minced ginger

1 teaspoon finely chopped chives

IN A SMALL BOWL, combine soy sauce, wine, orange zest, and ginger. Add the garlic, lemon zest, and peanut oil and mix well. Place the chicken wings in a sealable plastic bag, pour in the marinade, seal, and shake. Marinate overnight in the refrigerator.

REMOVE THE CHICKEN WINGS from the bag and grill over medium heat for approximately 20 minutes. Brush often with the marinade.

COMBINE ALL THE INGREDIENTS for the dip and mix well. Serve with the chicken wings and celery sticks. ◉

Most people prefer to cut off the wing tips prior to cooking, leaving just the two meatier pieces. Save the wing tips for chicken stock.

SERVES 4 TO 6

Chicken Wings Americana

Fritz Sonnenschmidt

Remember never to place raw meat in a hot marinade or it will start to cook and generate bacteria.

SERVES 4 TO 6

2 tablespoons oil

6 tablespoons sugar

¼ cup apple cider vinegar

¾ cup plus 2 tablespoons tomato ketchup

¾ cup plus 2 tablespoons chili or barbecue sauce

1 clove garlic, finely chopped

1 tablespoon honey

1 teaspoon freshly ground coffee

⅓ teaspoon mustard

2 pounds chicken wings (about 10 whole wings)

IN A MEDIUM SAUCEPAN, heat the oil and sugar and caramelize. Add the vinegar, ketchup, chili sauce, garlic, honey, coffee, and mustard and bring to a boil. Remove from the heat and chill in the refrigerator.

ONCE THE MARINADE is chilled, add the chicken wings and marinate for 3 to 4 hours or overnight. Remove the wings, place on the grill over medium heat, and grill for 20 minutes, turning occasionally. Brush often with the marinade. When the wings are nicely browned and cooked through, remove from heat and serve. ◉

Chicken Wings Asian Style

Fritz Sonnenschmidt

4 stalks lemongrass, tender bottoms only, finely chopped (approximately 1 cup),
    or zest of 2 lemons

⅓ cup light soy sauce

2 tablespoons sesame oil

2 tablespoons finely grated ginger

1 red chile pepper

1½ teaspoons curry powder

6 sprigs cilantro, chopped

2 pounds chicken wings (about 10 whole wings)

4 stalks celery, cut into 4-inch sticks

IN A LARGE BOWL, combine all ingredients except the chicken wings and celery and mix well. Add the wings and toss to coat. Place the wings and marinade in a sealable plastic bag. Marinate for 2 to 3 hours in the refrigerator, shaking the bag occasionally.

SPRAY THE GRILL with vegetable oil cooking spray. Place the celery sticks on the grill over medium heat for about 4 minutes. Remove and set aside.

REMOVE THE WINGS from the bag and grill over medium heat for 6 to 10 minutes on each side or to desired doneness. Serve with the grilled celery sticks. ◉

Lemongrass, an herb from Southeast Asia, has become increasingly popular in the United States. As its name suggests, it has a lemon flavor, which complements many dishes and is often found in Asian salads, soups, and seafood.

SERVES 4 TO 6

Chicken Wings Ming Style

Fritz Sonnenschmidt

This recipe has a delicious
sauce that is added
to the wings at
the end of cooking for
additional flavor.

SERVES 6

18 chicken wings (about 4 pounds)

5 tablespoons soy sauce

2 tablespoons dry sherry plus ¼ cup for thickening mixture

2 to 3 drops hot sauce

5 tablespoons vegetable oil

1 tablespoon sesame oil

1 teaspoon minced fresh ginger

1 scallion, chopped

⅓ teaspoon crushed red pepper flakes

1 teaspoon chile powder

½ cup chicken stock

2 tablespoons brown sugar

2 to 3 teaspoons cornstarch dissolved in sherry

Chinese cabbage leaves, for garnish

SEPARATE CHICKEN WINGS into sections. Combine 2 tablespoons of the soy sauce, 2 tablespoons sherry, hot sauce, 2 tablespoons vegetable oil, and the sesame oil in a medium dish. Add the wings, toss to coat, and marinate for 1 hour.

IN A MEDIUM SAUCEPAN over medium-high heat, heat the remaining 3 tablespoons of vegetable oil and sauté ginger and scallions for 1 minute. Add the pepper flakes, chili powder, chicken stock, the remaining 3 tablespoons soy sauce, and brown sugar and bring to a boil. Add the dissolved cornstarch and thicken the coating mixture.

REMOVE THE CHICKEN WINGS from the marinade and grill over medium heat for 15 minutes or until cooked. Toss the wings in the coating mixture and place on a platter on the grill for 2 to 3 minutes to dry. Remove from the grill, garnish with Chinese cabbage leaves and serve the remaining coating mixture as a dip. ◉

Mexican Shrimp Cocktail

Fritz Sonnenschmidt

1 pound ripe tomatoes, quartered

Kosher salt to taste

2½ tablespoons fresh orange juice

1 tablespoon fresh lime juice

1 teaspoon Worcestershire sauce

1 teaspoon grated horseradish

Black pepper to taste

1 cup tomato concassée (cubed tomatoes)

1 cucumber, peeled, seeded, and cubed

1 ripe avocado, peeled, seeded, and cubed

2 tablespoons finely chopped cilantro

1 pound large shrimp, peeled and deveined

1 tablespoon freshly ground coffee

⅓ teaspoon kosher salt or to taste

Olive oil

4 (3-inch-long) celery sticks with leaves, for garnish

4 lime wedges, for garnish

Grilled sourdough bread

PLACE THE QUARTERED TOMATOES in a large bowl. Season with salt and let stand for 2 hours. Place in a food processor and purée. Strain through cheesecloth and discard the pulp. Return the tomato juice to the bowl and add the orange juice, lime juice, Worcestershire sauce, horseradish, salt, and pepper. Mix well. Add the tomato concassée, cucumber, avocado, and cilantro and mix well.

SEASON THE PEELED SHRIMP with coffee, ⅓ teaspoon salt, and pepper. Spray with olive oil and grill over high heat for 2 minutes on each side or to desired doneness.

FILL 4 LARGE red wine glasses with the cocktail sauce. Top with the shrimps and garnish with celery sticks and lime wedges. Serve with grilled sourdough bread. ◑

The secret ingredient here is the use of coffee as a rub on the shrimp. It adds a wonderful flavor and rich color to the cooked shrimp.

SERVES 4

Pepper–Crusted Black and Blue Steak and Spicy Sesame Spinach with Soy–Wasabi Dipping Sauce

Chris Schlesinger | Reprinted from *How to Cook Meat*, HarperCollins Publishers

1 (2-pound) boneless strip loin steak, 2½ to 3½ inches thick

Kosher salt

¼ cup freshly cracked white pepper

Spicy Sesame Spinach

1 pound fresh spinach, trimmed and washed well

2 tablespoons Asian sesame oil

10 dashes Tabasco sauce

1 tablespoon sugar

Soy–Wasabi Dipping Sauce

½ cup soy sauce

2 tablespoons wasabi powder (available in Asian markets), mixed with water to the consistency of wet sand

4 ounces pickled ginger (available in Asian markets)

PAT THE STEAK dry with paper towels, then rub kosher salt and white pepper on all sides. On a hot grill, sear the steak well on the top and bottom and sides, about 4 minutes each. Remove the steak from the heat and allow to rest.

BRING A LARGE POT of salted water to a boil and fill your sink or a large bowl with ice and water. Blanch the spinach in the boiling water for 1 minute; do not overcook, or the spinach will lose its bright color and fresh taste. Drain and immediately plunge into the ice water to stop the cooking process, then drain again and squeeze dry by the handful. (Be sure the spinach is dry; if it's too moist, the final dish may be soggy.)

IN A SMALL BOWL, combine the oil, Tabasco sauce, and sugar and mix well. Add the spinach and mix well to coat the spinach with the dressing.

TO MAKE THE DIPPING SAUCE, combine the soy sauce and wasabi and mix well.

SLICE THE STEAK very thin on the bias, against the grain. Place a piece of pickled ginger and a bit of the spinach mixture on each slice of steak, then roll up tightly and pin together with a toothpick. Serve with the dipping sauce. ◉

This wonderful appetizer pops with the unique personalities of its ingredients, from the fresh cracked white pepper and pickled ginger to the soy and hot sauces. It calls for an especially thick cut of strip steak, which you will have to ask your butcher to custom cut.

SERVES 8 TO 10

Grilled Vegetarian Club Sandwich

Fritz Sonnenschmidt

4 red bell peppers

4 portobello mushrooms, about 4 inches wide, stems removed and gills scraped out

2 to 3 Japanese eggplant, cut in ¾-inch rounds

1 zucchini, cut into 8 (¾ inch) rounds

1 red onion, cut into ¼-inch-thick slices

Sesame oil

Salt and pepper to taste

1 teaspoon chopped fresh thyme

2 tablespoons balsamic vinegar

2 to 3 cloves garlic, grilled

¾ cup olive oil plus extra for brushing

12 slices white bread

4 tablespoons chopped fresh basil

GRILL THE RED PEPPERS over medium heat until charred. Place in a plastic bag and steam for 10 minutes. Peel under running water. Cut in half, remove the stems and seeds, and set aside.

BRUSH THE MUSHROOMS, eggplant, zucchini, and onions with sesame oil. Season with salt and pepper. Grill the vegetables on medium heat, turning twice: approximately 8 minutes for the mushrooms, 6 minutes for the eggplant, 3 minutes for the zucchini, and 4 minutes for the onion. Remove from the heat and place on a plate. Sprinkle with thyme.

PLACE 2 HALVES of the red pepper, balsamic vinegar, and grilled garlic in a blender. Add the olive oil and season with salt and pepper. Purée until smooth.

BRUSH THE BREAD SLICES with olive oil and grill over medium heat for 1 minute on each side. Divide the vegetables evenly on 8 slices of bread. Top with the red pepper sauce and sprinkle with basil. Stack a bread slice with vegetables on each of 4 slices with vegetables, and top these 4 sandwiches with the 4 remaining bread slices. Secure with toothpicks and slice in half. Serve with the leftover red pepper sauce. ◉

Japanese eggplant is smaller and thinner than regular eggplant. Look for ones that are firm and dark colored with a smooth and shiny skin.

SERVES 4

Grilled Pound Cake and Sweet Peach Napoleon with Crystal Cream

Marcel Desaulniers

When it comes to grilling, peaches have become a favorite among chefs. The turbinado sugar used in this recipe is a raw brown sugar that can be purchased at specialty food stores.

SERVES 4

1 teaspoon unsalted butter, melted, plus 1 cup (2 sticks), cut into 8 pieces

2½ cups cake flour

¼ teaspoon baking soda

½ teaspoon salt

1½ cups granulated sugar

3 large eggs

⅓ cup whole milk

1 teaspoon pure vanilla extract

4 medium peaches

1 cup heavy cream

¼ cup turbinado sugar

PREHEAT THE OVEN to 325°F. Lightly coat the inside of a 9 by 5 by 3–inch nonstick loaf pan with the 1 teaspoon of melted butter. Set aside.

SIFT TOGETHER the cake flour, baking soda, and salt onto a large piece of parchment or waxed paper. Set aside until needed.

PLACE THE GRANULATED SUGAR and 1 cup butter in the bowl of an electric mixer fitted with a paddle. Mix on low speed for 2 minutes, then beat on medium for 3 minutes. Scrape down the sides of the bowl and the paddle. Beat for an additional 3 minutes on medium speed. Scrape down the sides of the bowl, then beat for 2 minutes on high speed until soft and slightly fluffy. Scrape down the sides of the bowl. Add 3 eggs, one at a time, beating on medium for 30 seconds after each addition. Scrape down the sides of the bowl once all the eggs have been incorporated.

NOW BEAT on medium speed for 4 minutes until very fluffy. Scrape down the sides of the bowl. On low speed, gradually add one-third of the milk followed by one-third of the sifted dry ingredients. Once these ingredients have been incorporated, repeat twice more, adding a third of the ingredients each time. Mix on low to incorporate for 30 seconds. Add the vanilla extract and beat on medium for 15 seconds until combined. Remove the bowl from the mixer and finish mixing the batter until thoroughly combined. Transfer the batter to the prepared loaf pan, spreading evenly. Bake on the center rack of the oven until a toothpick inserted in the center of the cake comes out clean, about 1 hour and 15 minutes to 1 hour and 20 minutes. Remove the cake from the oven and cool in the pan at room temperature for 15 to 20 minutes. Turn the cake out of the pan onto a baking sheet. Turn the cake top side up, then refrigerate for 1 hour.

PARE 1/4 INCH off the tops and bottoms of each of the peaches. Cut the peaches in half horizontally and remove the pits. Cut the peach halves in half horizontally once more. Grill the fruit over a medium-hot fire until well charred, about 2 minutes on each side. Transfer the grilled peaches to the upper rack of the grill and keep warm.

PLACE THE COOLED CAKE on a clean, dry work surface. Cut 3/4-inch-thick slices of the cake. Grill the slices over medium-low heat for about 1½ to 2 minutes on each side, rotating the cake frequently for even grilling. Keep warm.

PLACE THE HEAVY CREAM in the bowl of an electric mixer fitted with a balloon whip. Whisk on high speed until soft peaks form, about 1½ to 2 minutes. Add the turbinado sugar and whisk to combine, about 10 seconds.

PLACE A SLICE of grilled cake in the center of individual plates. Top the cake with 1 tablespoon of the whipped cream and some grilled peach slices. Repeat this process with the remaining peaches and slices of grilled cake. Use any remaining whipped cream to garnish the plates. ◉

Pecan and Brown Sugar Crescents with Grilled Peaches in Blue Cheese Cabernet Sauvignon

Fritz Sonnenschmidt

Pecan and Brown Sugar Crescents

1 cup flour

¾ cup pecans

½ cup butter, cut into ½-inch pieces

¼ cup brown sugar

1 teaspoon vanilla extract

½ teaspoon ground cinnamon

Pinch of salt

Confectioners' sugar, for dusting

Grilled Peaches

1 cup cabernet sauvignon

2 tablespoons granulated sugar

1 teaspoon freshly ground pepper

3 peaches, halved and pitted

2 tablespoons virgin olive oil

4 ounces blue cheese, crumbled, for garnish

Mint leaves, for garnish

PLACE ALL CRESCENT ingredients (except the confectioners' sugar) in a food processor and process until the mixture comes together as a dough. Roll 1 heaping tablespoon of dough between your palms to form a 2½–inch–long rope tapering at the ends. Place on an ungreased baking sheet and curl the

continued on next page

This makes an unbeatable combination—buttery, delicate cookies, grilled sweet peaches, rich cabernet, and tangy blue cheese.

MAKES APPROXIMATELY 25 CRESCENTS

Pecan and Brown Sugar Crescents with Grilled Peaches in Blue Cheese Cabernet Sauvignon (continued)

ends to form a crescent. Continue with the remaining dough, placing the crescents about 1 inch apart on the baking sheet. Grill the sheet of crescents over low heat for 15 to 20 minutes. Remove and allow to cool. Dust with confectioners' sugar.

IN A SMALL SAUCEPAN, combine the cabernet with the sugar and the pepper. Bring to a boil and reduce by two-thirds, 45 to 60 minutes, or until syrupy.

RUB THE PEACHES with the olive oil and grill over high heat until lightly colored. Brush with wine sauce and grill for 1 more minute. Place on a plate. Dribble the wine sauce over the peaches and garnish with the blue cheese. Decorate with mint leaves and serve with the crescents. ◉

Fresh Fruit from the Grill

Fritz Sonnenschmidt

1 cup fresh orange juice

⅓ cup balsamic vinegar

½ cup sugar

½ cup butter, melted

½ cup white zinfandel

1 pear, cut into quarters

1 orange, cut into ¼-inch-thick slices

1 banana, peeled and cut in half

1 peach, pitted and cut in half

2 apricots, pitted and cut in half

Sliced French bread (optional)

Vanilla ice cream (optional)

IN A LARGE SHALLOW BOWL, combine the orange juice, vinegar, sugar, butter, and white zinfandel. Add the fruit and carefully toss to coat. Let the fruit stand in this marinade for 20 minutes.

DRAIN THE FRUIT and transfer the marinade to a small saucepan. Grill the fruit over medium–high heat for 1 to 2 minutes per side. While the fruit is grilling, bring the marinade to a boil and then remove from the heat.

DIVIDE THE GRILLED FRUIT mixture among 4 to 6 dessert bowls and pour the hot marinade over the fruit. Serve warm with French bread or ice cream. ◉

If you have never tried grilling fruit, after trying this recipe, you may never stop. The marinade is delicious and easy to make and will bring out the naturally sweet fruit flavors.

SERVES 4 TO 6

Sides and Salads

A Panoply of Grilled Mushrooms, Asparagus, and Artichokes in a Rosemary-Scented Tomato Broth

Marcel Desaulniers

4 medium plum tomatoes (2 ounces), washed, cored, and halved lengthwise

6 tablespoons extra virgin olive oil

Salt and freshly cracked black pepper to taste

1 cup well-seasoned vegetable stock

1 (4- to 5-inch) stem fresh rosemary

24 spears fresh asparagus

4 large artichokes

1 tablespoon fresh lemon juice

1 (4- to 6-ounce) fresh oyster mushroom cluster

12 medium shiitake mushroom caps

4 large portobello mushroom caps

BRUSH THE TOMATOES with 1 tablespoon olive oil and season with salt and pepper. Grill the tomato halves, cut side down, over medium–high heat until nicely charred, about 4 minutes. Turn and grill them on the round side for about 1 minute. Remove the tomatoes from the grill and cut each half into quarters. Transfer the cut tomatoes to a medium pot. Add the vegetable stock and rosemary and bring to a simmer. Season with salt and pepper. Remove the pot from the heat and keep warm.

CUT ¼ INCH OFF the bottoms of the asparagus and lightly peel the ends of each spear. Bring 3 quarts of salted water to a boil in a 5–quart saucepan over high heat. Add the asparagus and cook until tender, about 3 minutes depending on the thickness of the asparagus. Drain the asparagus, then immediately plunge into ice water to stop the cooking and keep the asparagus bright green. Drain thoroughly and set aside.

continued on next page

Here's an exciting vegetarian meal to make outdoors. All the vegetables benefit remarkably from their time on the grill, resulting in a dish that explodes with flavors.

SERVES 4

A Panoply of Grilled Mushrooms, Asparagus, and Artichokes in a Rosemary-Scented Tomato Broth (continued)

AGAIN, BRING 3 QUARTS of salted water to a boil in a 5-quart saucepan over high heat. Remove the outer leaves from the artichokes. Slice off the top third of the artichoke. Using a sharp-edged spoon, scrape out the fuzzy thistle from the center of each. Cut away all but ¼ inch of each stem. Place the artichokes, as soon as they are cut, into 2 quarts of cold water mixed with the lemon juice. Keep them in the acidulated water for only a few minutes, then drain and add to the salted boiling water. Boil the artichokes until cooked through, when easily pierced by a skewer, about 20 to 25 minutes. Drain the cooked artichokes, then immediately plunge into ice water. Drain well and peel the fibrous outer layer from the artichokes. Set aside.

LIGHTLY BRUSH the asparagus, artichokes, and mushrooms with the remaining 5 tablespoons olive oil. Season with salt and pepper. Grill the asparagus over medium-high heat for 3 to 4 minutes until nicely charred. Transfer to a deep serving tray or bowl. Grill the artichokes over medium-high heat for about 2 minutes on each side until nicely charred. Transfer these to the tray or bowl. Finally, grill the mushrooms over medium-high heat for about 3 to 4 minutes on each side until nicely charred. Artfully arrange the grilled mushrooms with the artichokes and asparagus. Pour the hot tomato broth over the vegetables and serve immediately. ◉

Tommy's Red Cabbage Salad with Grilled Pineapple in Spicy Sesame-Lime Dressing

Chris Schlesinger | Reprinted from *Lettuce in Your Kitchen*, William Morrow and Company

Spicy Sesame-Lime Dressing

½ cup fresh orange juice (from about 1 large orange)

¼ cup fresh lime juice (from about 2 medium limes)

¼ cup sesame oil

6 tablespoons rice wine vinegar or white vinegar

¼ cup molasses

2 tablespoons minced fresh ginger

9 dashes Tabasco sauce

2 tablespoons crushed star anise, or 1 tablespoon five-spice powder

¼ cup roughly chopped cilantro

Salt and freshly cracked black pepper to taste

Red Cabbage Salad

¼ cup butter

¼ cup light or dark brown sugar

1 medium pineapple, peeled and sliced into rounds about 1 inch thick (about 8 rounds)

1 medium head red cabbage, cored and cut into thin strips

1½ cups shredded carrots (about 2 medium carrots)

1 bunch scallions, white and green parts trimmed and thinly sliced

IN A SMALL BOWL, combine all the dressing ingredients and mix well. Set aside.

IN A SMALL SAUCEPAN, melt the butter over very low heat. Add the brown sugar, stir well to combine, and remove from heat. Grill the pineapple rounds over medium-high heat until nicely browned, 2 to 3 minutes per side. During the last minute of cooking, brush the top sides liberally with the butter-sugar glaze. Remove from the grill and cut each round into eighths.

IN A LARGE BOWL, combine the pineapple with the cabbage, carrots, and scallions. Stir the dressing well, add just enough to moisten the ingredients (you will have some dressing left over), toss well, and serve. ◉

Grilled pineapple is a wonderful treat, whether it's for a salad as in this case, as an accompaniment for a main dish, or as dessert. This salad's dressing is also excellent over grilled chicken wings or as a barbecue sauce with pork.

SERVES 8 TO 10

Arugula and Radicchio with Grilled Mozzarella and Bread Skewers with Basil-Pine Nut Dressing

Chris Schlesinger | Reprinted from *Lettuce in Your Kitchen*, William Morrow and Company

Basil-Pine Nut Dressing

¼ cup pine nuts, toasted in a 350°F oven for 7 to 10 minutes until golden

4 cloves garlic, peeled

1 cup loosely packed fresh basil leaves

¼ cup grainy mustard

1½ cups olive oil

¼ cup red wine vinegar

¼ cup fresh lemon juice (from about 1 large lemon)

Salt and freshly ground black pepper to taste

Salad

1 pound fresh mozzarella, diced large (about 16 pieces)

16 (1-inch) squares good-quality day-old baguette or peasant bread

Salt and freshly cracked black pepper to taste

3 bunches arugula, trimmed, washed, and dried

2 heads radicchio, outer leaves discarded, inner leaves cored and sliced very thin

3 medium tomatoes, cored and quartered

½ cup kalamata or other briny black olives (optional)

COMBINE THE PINE NUTS, garlic, basil, and mustard in a blender and purée. With the motor running, add the oil in a steady stream. Stop, add the vinegar and lemon juice, and pulse to blend. Season with salt and pepper. Set aside.

ALTERNATE THE MOZZARELLA and bread cubes on skewers and season with salt and pepper. Grill over medium heat until the bread is nicely browned and the cheese begins to melt, 2 to 3 minutes per side.

IN A LARGE BOWL, combine the remaining ingredients. Stir the dressing well, add just enough to moisten the salad (you will have dressing left over), and toss to coat. Top the salad with the mozzarella and bread cubes and serve. ◉

Be sure to use fresh mozzarella, a mild, unsalted white cow's milk cheese that comes packed in water. It is widely available now, but can always be found in Italian food stores.

SERVES 8 TO 10

The inspiration for this dish came from one of Boston's most famous chefs, Jasper White, and his duck and papaya salad. This dressing is also delicious on any kind of grilled game bird or even a thick steak.

SERVES 4 TO 6

Arugula and Duck Salad with Mango, Caramelized Onions, and Spiced Pecans with Cumberland Vinaigrette

Chris Schlesinger | Reprinted from *Lettuce in Your Kitchen*, William Morrow and Company

Cumberland Vinaigrette

½ cup port wine

⅓ cup apricot jam

1 teaspoon minced lime zest (no white)

1 teaspoon minced orange zest (no white)

½ cup olive oil

¼ cup balsamic vinegar

Salt and freshly cracked black pepper to taste

Arugula and Duck Salad

1 tablespoon olive oil

7 dashes Tabasco sauce

½ cup whole pecan halves

4 (8-ounce) duck breasts, boneless

Salt and freshly cracked black pepper

16 red onion slices

2 bunches arugula, trimmed, washed, and dried

2 mangoes, peeled, pitted, and diced large

1 red bell pepper, seeded, cored, and cut into thin strips

IN A SMALL SAUCEPAN, combine the port, apricot jam, and lime and orange zests and cook over medium heat, stirring, until the jam has melted. Increase the heat to high and stir until the mixture starts to boil, then reduce to low and simmer, stirring frequently to prevent burning, until the mixture has been reduced by about two–thirds, about 30 minutes. Remove from heat and cool to room temperature. Add the oil and vinegar, stir to combine, season with salt and pepper, and set aside.

PREHEAT THE OVEN to 350°F.

IN A SMALL BOWL, combine the olive oil and Tabasco, and mix well. Toss the pecans with this mixture, spread on a baking sheet, and toast in the oven until nicely browned, 12 to 15 minutes. Remove from the oven and set aside to cool. Keep oven on.

SPRINKLE THE DUCK BREASTS with salt and pepper and place in a large sauté pan, fat side down. Cook over medium–high heat until well browned, 4 to 5 minutes per side. Remove from the pan and grill over medium heat for 5 minutes for medium–rare. Remove from the grill and set aside for 5 minutes.

MEANWHILE, DRAIN all but about 3 tablespoons of duck fat from the sauté pan, add the onions, and sauté over medium–high heat, stirring frequently, until well browned, 7 to 10 minutes. Remove from the heat and place in a large bowl.

ADD THE ARUGULA, mangoes, and peppers to the bowl with the caramelized onions. Stir the dressing well, add just enough dressing to moisten the salad ingredients (you will have some dressing left over), and toss to coat. Place the salad on individual plates. Slice the duck breast into thin slices and lay them on top of the salads. Sprinkle with the spicy pecans and serve. ◉

Country Corn and Scallop Luncheon Salad

Fritz Sonnenschmidt

Here's a great way to grill corn: Soak the corn *with* its husk in water for several hours. Place on the grill and cook for 20 minutes or until tender. The husks will get very brown, but the corn will not char.

SERVES 4

1 pound salt (or Red Bliss) potatoes

2 to 3 tablespoons olive oil

2 ears corn, husks and silk removed

9 red onions, sliced ¼ inch thick

1 pound large scallops

Salt and pepper

Orange Bread

4 slices French or Italian baguette bread

¼ cup frozen orange juice concentrate, softened

3 tablespoons grated orange zest

Dressing

1 teaspoon mustard

¼ cup olive oil

1 tablespoon orange zest (from 1 orange)

Juice of 1 orange

2 to 3 tablespoons plain vinegar

½ teaspoon salt or more to taste

Freshly ground black pepper

½ pound mesclun mixture

CUT THE POTATOES in half. Brush with olive oil and grill over medium heat for 15 to 20 minutes or until tender. Place in a large bowl.

GRILL THE CORN over medium heat. Remove, allow to cool, and cut the kernels from the cobs. Add the corn to the potatoes.

BRUSH THE RED ONIONS with olive oil and grill over medium heat for 2 minutes on each side. Set aside.

SEASON THE SCALLOPS with salt and pepper. Brush with olive oil and grill on a high rack over medium heat for 1 minute each side.

TO MAKE THE ORANGE BREAD, on both sides brush the bread slices with orange juice. Sprinkle with the grated orange zest. Spray with olive oil and grill for 2 minutes each side.

IN A SMALL BOWL, combine all the dressing ingredients and mix well. Toss the mesclun with the potatoes and corn in some of the dressing and place in the center of a serving plate. Toss the scallops with the remaining dressing and arrange around the mesclun mixture. Decorate with grilled onions and serve with orange bread. ◉

Grilled Vegetable Medley with Blue Cheese Butter

Fritz Sonnenschmidt

¾ cup crumbled blue cheese

6 tablespoons soft butter

1 teaspoon fresh lemon juice

Salt and pepper to taste

2 tablespoons virgin olive oil

1 tablespoon freshly chopped basil

3 cloves garlic, roasted and mashed

2 pounds vegetables, such as asparagus, zucchini, yellow squash, carrots, and
    eggplants, peeled, trimmed, and sliced

IN A SMALL BOWL, blend blue cheese, butter, and lemon juice thoroughly. Season with salt and pepper. Cover with plastic wrap and refrigerate until ready to serve.

IN A BLENDER, combine olive oil, basil, and roasted garlic and blend until smooth. Pour over the vegetables. Season with salt and pepper and marinate for 20 minutes. Grill the vegetables over high heat and char on all sides, approximately 4 minutes each.

REMOVE TO A SERVING DISH and top with the prepared butter. ◉

Don't be afraid to experiment with grilling different kinds of vegetables. You may want to partially cook ahead of time the ones that take a longer time to reach doneness, such as potatoes or carrots.

SERVES 6

Dr. Hibachi's Spinach Salad with Grilled Lamb

Chris Schlesinger | Reprinted from *Lettuce in Your Kitchen*, William Morrow and Company

You can substitute romaine lettuce for the spinach in the salad. Watch the garlic carefully as it cooks to make sure it doesn't burn.

SERVES 4

Honey-Sage Dressing

½ cup plus 2 tablespoons olive oil

4 large cloves garlic, peeled and thinly sliced

3 tablespoons balsamic vinegar

1 tablespoon fresh lemon juice

2 teaspoons honey

1½ tablespoons minced fresh sage or mint

Salt and freshly cracked black pepper to taste

Salad

4 small loin or rib lamb chops, each about 1½ inches thick

Salt and freshly cracked black pepper

10 ounces spinach, trimmed, washed, and dried

3 roasted red peppers, seeded, cored, and cut into long, thin strips

1 red onion, halved and thinly sliced

¼ cup pine nuts, toasted in a 350°F oven, stirred frequently until golden about 10 minutes

IN A SMALL SAUTÉ PAN, heat ½ cup olive oil over medium heat until hot but not smoking. Add the garlic slices and sauté, stirring constantly to prevent burning, until they are light brown, about 2 minutes. Remove the garlic with a slotted spoon and drain on paper towels. Pour the oil into a small bowl and allow to cool. Add enough oil to make a ½ cup, then add the vinegar, lemon juice, honey, and sage and mix well. Season with salt and pepper and set aside.

SPRINKLE LAMB CHOPS with salt and pepper and grill over medium-high heat for 6 to 7 minutes for medium-rare; or continue to grill, checking every few minutes, until they are slightly less done than you like them.

IN A LARGE BOWL, combine the spinach, roasted peppers, and onion. Stir the dressing well, add just enough to moisten the salad (you will have dressing left over), and toss to coat. Place the salad on individual plates, top with a lamb chop, sprinkle with garlic chips and toasted pine nuts, and serve. ◉

Vegetarian Lentil Pie

Fritz Sonnenschmidt

1 ½ cups flour

½ cup butter

½ cup ice water

½ teaspoon salt

2 red bell peppers, cut in small dice

2 red chiles, cut in small dice

2 cloves garlic, minced

2 onions, minced

1 pound potatoes, cut in small dice

11 ounces lentils, washed and blanched

1 teaspoon chopped fresh thyme

1 teaspoon curry powder

3 tablespoons tomato paste, or 5 tablespoons tomato ketchup

1 pint vegetable stock

Salt to taste

1 tablespoon oil

1 ounce sunflower seeds

WITH A PASTRY BLENDER or fork, blend flour and butter to resemble coarse meal. Add the ice water and salt and knead into a pie dough. Refrigerate for 1 hour.

IN A LARGE BOWL, combine all the vegetables, lentils, thyme, curry powder, tomato paste, and vegetable stock. Mix well and season with salt.

ROLL OUT THE PIE DOUGH and cut out 2 round pie crusts. Place the bottom crust in a 9-inch pie plate. Fill with the lentil mixture. Cover with the top crust and seal and crimp the edges. Brush with oil and sprinkle with sunflowers seeds.

GRILL THE PIE over medium–high heat for 30 minutes. Reduce the grill heat to low and grill for 1 hour. Remove the pie from the grill and allow to rest for 10 minutes before serving. ◉

Modern gas grills, like the ones made by Weber, are so easy to use and reliable that it's possible to make delicious pies like these outdoors.

SERVES 4

Grilled Asparagus Salad with Grilled Swiss Cheese and Prosciutto

Fritz Sonnenschmidt

This makes an elegant and unusual luncheon dish. Try to get the highest quality and tastiest prosciutto and Swiss cheese you can find as they dominate the dish.

SERVES 4

¼ cup balsamic vinegar

1 cup finely chopped shallots

1 teaspoon sugar

1 cup olive oil plus extra for brushing

Salt and freshly cracked black pepper to taste

1½ pounds asparagus, peeled and trimmed

4 (3-ounce) sticks Swiss cheese, each 1½ inches thick

1 (5-ounce) bag of mixed greens

8 slices prosciutto

3 tablespoons crystallized walnuts (nuts cooked in a simple syrup until liquid evaporates and then coated with a little oil to prevent sticking)

Grilled garlic bread

IN A MEDIUM BOWL, combine the vinegar, shallots, and sugar. While the sugar is dissolving, whisk in 1 cup olive oil. Season with salt and pepper. Place the asparagus in a shallow dish and drizzle with approximately 2 tablespoons of the marinade. Season the asparagus with salt and pepper and grill over medium–high heat until crisp, approximately 3 to 6 minutes. Remove the asparagus to the shallow dish with the rest of the marinade.

BRUSH THE SWISS CHEESE with olive oil and sprinkle with black pepper. Grill over high heat for 1 minute on each side.

REMOVE THE ASPARAGUS from the marinade and arrange on individual plates. Toss the mixed greens in the marinade left in the shallow dish. Top the asparagus with the greens and decorate with the grilled cheese and prosciutto. Serve with grilled garlic bread. ◉

Poultry

Grilled Skewers of Ginger Chicken with Fennel and Sweet Bell Peppers

Marcel Desaulniers

¼ cup soy sauce

1 tablespoon sugar

2 teaspoons grated fresh ginger

½ teaspoon cayenne pepper

2 pounds boneless, skinless chicken breasts, cut into 1-inch cubes

2 fennel bulbs (about 1½ pounds), tops removed and washed

Salt and freshly ground black pepper to taste

3 tablespoons cider vinegar

1 tablespoon Dijon mustard

½ teaspoon fresh chopped rosemary

½ cup extra virgin olive oil

4 large bell peppers, 1 each of red, green, yellow, and orange, washed, cored, seeded, membrane removed, and quartered lengthwise

IN A MEDIUM BOWL, whisk together the soy sauce, sugar, ginger, and cayenne pepper. Add the chicken cubes and gently toss to combine. Cover tightly with plastic wrap and refrigerate for 1 hour.

CUT THE FENNEL BULBS into quarters lengthwise. Season with salt and pepper. Grill over medium–low heat for 7 to 9 minutes on each side. Transfer the fennel to the upper rack of the grill to finish cooking.

IN A MEDIUM BOWL, whisk together the cider vinegar, mustard, and rosemary. Whisk in the olive oil in a slow, steady stream until incorporated. Season with salt and pepper and whisk to combine. Cover with plastic wrap and set aside.

INCREASE THE GRILL HEAT to medium–hot. Season the peppers with salt and pepper and grill for 5 minutes on each side. Transfer them and the fennel to the bowl of vinaigrette. Toss to combine and keep warm while grilling the chicken.

DIVIDE THE CHICKEN into 4 equal portions onto skewers. Grill over a medium fire for 10 minutes, turning frequently to brown evenly. Mound the grilled fennel and peppers on individual plates. Remove the chicken from the skewers and place on the vegetables. Serve immediately. ◉

If you haven't tried it, grilling fennel is wonderful—it brings out the sweet, fragrant flavors. Avoid fennel bulbs that show signs of browning.

SERVES 4

Pepper-Charred Boneless Quail with Crisp Apple Slaw and Warm Smoked Bacon Dressing

Marcel Desaulniers

Quail is a tasty game bird that is readily available in most parts of the country. Ask your butcher to debone it for you.

SERVES 4

½ pound hickory-smoked slab bacon

2 tablespoons cider vinegar

½ cup vegetable oil

2½ cups well-seasoned chicken stock, heated

1 cup wild rice

Salt and freshly cracked black pepper to taste

1 tablespoon clover honey

2 tablespoons raspberry vinegar

2 Granny Smith apples, washed and dried

2 Red Delicious apples, washed and dried

1 small red onion, peeled, core removed, sliced lengthwise into ⅛-inch-thick slices

2 scallions, washed, ends trimmed, and sliced on the bias

8 whole quail, partially boned

PREHEAT THE OVEN to 325°F.

TRIM THE RIND from the bacon and cut it into ¼-inch pieces. Transfer to a wire rack over a baking sheet with sides. Cook on the center rack of the oven for 10 to 12 minutes, until golden brown. Remove the bacon from the oven and transfer to paper towels to drain. Save the liquefied bacon fat on the baking sheet for the quail. While the bacon is draining, combine the cider vinegar and vegetable oil in a medium bowl. Whisk vigorously until combined. Add the warm bacon and stir to combine. Set aside.

IN THE TOP of a double boiler over medium heat, add the hot chicken stock and wild rice. Season lightly with salt and pepper and cover tightly. Cook the rice for about 1 hour until cooked but slightly firm to the bite. Strain the chicken stock from the rice and transfer the rice to a large bowl. Add the bacon dressing and stir to coat. Adjust the seasoning and keep warm.

WHISK TOGETHER the honey and raspberry vinegar in a medium bowl. Use a mandoline to cut the apples into thin spaghetti–like strands the length of the apple and ⅛ inch wide. Immediately toss the apples with the honey and vinegar mixture. Add the sliced red onions and scallions. Toss to combine. Season with salt and pepper. Set aside while charring the quail.

LIGHTLY COAT each of the quail with some of the leftover bacon fat. Generously season with salt and pepper. Char the quail over a hot fire on all sides for about 5 to 6 minutes, until slightly blackened. Divide the warm wild rice with bacon dressing in the center of each plate and create a small well in the center for the apple slaw. Place the apple slaw in the well of the rice and a charred quail on the apple slaw and serve immediately. ◉

Herb-Grilled Chicken Breast with Pineapple Basmati Rice and Pink Grapefruit Butter

Marcel Desaulniers

Pink Grapefruit Butter

1 large pink grapefruit, peeled and sectioned

½ cup unsalted butter, softened

1 teaspoon grenadine

½ teaspoon freshly cracked black pepper

Pineapple Basmati Rice

2 teaspoons vegetable oil

2 tablespoons minced red onion

Salt and pepper to taste

1 cup white basmati rice

1¾ cups fresh, well-seasoned chicken stock, heated

1 cup diced fresh pineapple

4 (6-ounce) chicken breasts, with skin

1½ tablespoons olive oil

Salt and freshly cracked black pepper

½ teaspoon chopped fresh parsley

¼ teaspoon chopped fresh basil

¼ teaspoon chopped fresh oregano

¼ teaspoon chopped fresh rosemary

¼ teaspoon chopped fresh thyme

½ cup toasted macadamia nuts, chopped into ¼-inch pieces

continued on next page

Basmati rice is a tasty aromatic rice from India and Pakistan. Here it's made pilaf style with chicken broth and onions, then served with pineapple and macadamia nuts for an unbeatable combination.

SERVES 4

Herb–Grilled Chicken Breast with Pineapple Basmati Rice, and Pink Grapefruit Butter (continued)

CUT THE INDIVIDUAL SECTIONS of the grapefruit into ¼–inch pieces and place in a small bowl. Add the soft butter, grenadine, and black pepper to the fruit. Mix until well blended. Set aside.

HEAT THE VEGETABLE OIL in a medium saucepan over medium–high heat. Add the onions, season with salt and pepper, and cook until the onions are tender, about 2 minutes. Add the rice and stir to coat with the oil. Add the chicken stock and stir to blend. Increase the heat to high and bring to a boil. As soon as the stock boils, cover, reduce the heat to medium, and continue to cook the rice until tender, about 15 minutes. Transfer the rice to a large bowl. Add the pineapple and stir to combine. Adjust the seasoning and keep warm.

PLACE THE CHICKEN breasts in a medium bowl. Drizzle the olive oil over the breasts. Season with salt and black pepper. Add the chopped herbs and mix until each breast is well coated with herbs. Grill the breasts over a medium fire for 4 to 5 minutes on each side. Transfer the breasts to the upper rack of the grill to finish cooking while you arrange the plates.

PILE THE PINEAPPLE RICE in the center of each plate. Place the chicken on top of the rice. Top with grapefruit butter, sprinkle each plate with the chopped macadamia nuts, and serve immediately. ◉

Grilled Turkey Scaloppine with Fire-Roasted Corn, Grilled Tomatoes, and Spinach Cream

Marcel Desaulniers

4 large ears fresh corn, husk on, soaked in cold water for 1 hour

Salt and freshly ground black pepper to taste

2 teaspoons unsalted butter

1 tablespoon minced shallots

¾ cup spinach leaves, washed, dried, and finely chopped

1¼ cups heavy cream

Freshly ground nutmeg to taste

6 medium to large plum tomatoes (4 ounces), washed, cored, and halved lengthwise

1 tablespoon extra virgin olive oil

1 pound boneless, skinless white turkey breast

REMOVE THE CORN from the water and shake to remove some of the water. Place the corn over a hot fire to roast until tender and slightly golden brown, about 20 to 25 minutes. Remove the roasted corn from the grill. Remove the husk and the silk from the ears. Cut the kernels from the cobs. Season the kernels with salt and pepper and keep warm.

WHILE THE CORN is roasting, heat the butter in a medium saucepan. Add the shallots, season with salt and pepper, and sauté for 2 minutes, stirring frequently. Add the chopped spinach, stir to incorporate, and cook for 1 minute. Add the heavy cream and bring to a boil. Reduce the heat and simmer, stirring frequently, until a sauce forms, about 15 minutes. Adjust the seasoning with salt, pepper, and freshly ground nutmeg. Keep warm.

continued on next page

Scaloppine is the Italian word for cutlet; in French it's called *escalope*. Remember to pound the cutlets to an even thickness so that the meat cooks evenly.

SERVES 4

Grilled Turkey Scaloppine with Fire-Roasted Corn, Grilled Tomatoes, and Spinach Cream (continued)

BRUSH THE TOMATOES with the olive oil and season with salt and pepper. Grill the tomato halves, cut side down, until nicely charred, about 4 minutes. Turn and grill them on the round side for about 1 minute. Transfer the tomato halves to the top rack of the grill to finish cooking while you grill the turkey.

SLICING ACROSS the grain, cut the turkey into sixteen 1-ounce pieces. Place a turkey slice on a sheet of plastic wrap. Cover with more plastic wrap, then use a meat cleaver or the bottom of a sauté pan to slightly flatten the turkey. Remove and discard the plastic wrap and set aside the turkey slice. Repeat until all the slices have been flattened into scaloppine.

SEASON THE TURKEY on both sides with salt and pepper. Quickly grill the turkey over medium-high heat, about 1 to 1½ minutes for each side. Remove from the grill and keep warm.

EVENLY SPREAD the sauce on 4 plates. Place a mound of corn in the center of each plate followed by 3 grilled tomato halves outlining the corn. Place the turkey scaloppines on the corn mounds and serve immediately. ◉

Grilled West Indies Spice-Rubbed Chicken Breast with Grilled Banana

Chris Schlesinger | Reprinted from *The Thrill of the Grill*, William Morrow and Company

Spice Rub

3 tablespoons curry powder

3 tablespoons ground cumin

2 tablespoons allspice

3 tablespoons paprika

2 tablespoons powdered ginger

1 tablespoon cayenne pepper

2 tablespoons salt

2 tablespoons freshly cracked black pepper

4 boneless chicken breasts, with skin

4 firm bananas, unpeeled and halved lengthwise

2 tablespoons vegetable oil

1 tablespoon soft butter

2 tablespoons molasses

Juice from 2 limes

MIX ALL THE SPICES together well, rub this mixture over both sides of each chicken breast, cover and refrigerate for 2 hours.

GRILL THE CHICKEN BREASTS, skin side down, over medium heat for 7 to 8 minutes, until well browned and heavily crusted. Turn them and grill 10 minutes more. To check for doneness, cut into the largest breast at the fattest point to be sure the meat is opaque with no red. Remove the chicken from the grill.

RUB THE BANANA HALVES with vegetable oil and place them on the grill, flat side down. Grill them for about 2 minutes, or until slightly golden in color. Flip them and grill for an additional 2 minutes. Remove the banana halves from the grill. Mix the butter and molasses together and paint this over the bananas. Serve the chicken breasts and banana halves together, sprinkled with a little lime juice. ◉

This rub creates a distinctive, flavorful crust over a moist chicken breast. The grilled banana provides a nice touch of sweetness to contrast the crispy chicken. Remember not to overcook the chicken breast or it will be dry.

SERVES 4

Corn Bread–Stuffed Barbecue Game Hens with Bourbon–Shallot Sauce

Chris Schlesinger | Reprinted from *License to Grill,* William Morrow and Company

Corn Bread Stuffing

½ cup (1 stick) unsalted butter

1 large onion, peeled and finely diced

2 Granny Smith or other green apples, peeled, halved, cored, and finely diced

2 cups corn bread crumbled into small chunks

¼ cup roughly chopped fresh sage, oregano, and/or marjoram

1 cup milk

Salt and freshly ground black pepper to taste

Spice Rub

¼ cup paprika

¼ cup freshly cracked black pepper

¼ cup lightly packed brown sugar

¼ cup kosher salt

4 Rock Cornish game hens

Bourbon–Shallot Sauce

2 tablespoons olive oil

½ cup minced shallots

1 tablespoon minced garlic

2 cups chicken stock

1 cup bourbon

¼ cup fresh lemon juice (from about 1 lemon)

Salt and freshly ground black pepper to taste

continued on next page

Game hens are nifty for entertaining since each person gets a whole one and you don't have to bother with carving up portions. Remember to cook these game hens slowly on indirect heat.

SERVES 4

Corn Bread–Stuffed Barbecue Game Hens with Bourbon–Shallot Sauce (continued)

PLACE THE BUTTER and onion in a medium sauté pan over medium heat and sauté, stirring occasionally, until the onions are transparent, 5 to 7 minutes. Add the apples and sauté, stirring occasionally, for 5 minutes more. Transfer to a medium bowl, add the corn bread, herbs, milk, salt, and pepper, and mix well.

IN A SMALL BOWL, combine the spice rub ingredients and mix well. Divide the stuffing into 4 portions and stuff each bird, then cover each bird with the spice rub.

BUILD A SMALL FIRE off to one side of a covered grill, using enough charcoal to fill a shoebox. Let all the fuel become completely engulfed in flames and then, when the flames have died down and you are left with flickering coals, place the hens on the grill surface over the side with no fire. It is important that the flames not contact the hens at any time during cooking.

COVER THE GRILL and open the vents slightly. You will need to check the fire every 20 minutes or so as the hens cook, adding a bit more fuel as necessary to keep the fire going, for 1 to 1½ hours. To check for doneness, pierce a thigh of a hen with a fork. If the juices run clear, the hens are done.

IN A MEDIUM SAUCEPAN over high heat, heat the oil until hot but not smoking. Add the shallots and garlic and sauté, stirring occasionally, until soft, 3 to 5 minutes. Add the stock and bourbon and bring to a boil, then turn the heat to low and simmer until the liquid has reduced by about half, 30 to 45 minutes. Add the lemon juice and salt and pepper to taste, cook for 10 more minutes, and remove from heat.

WHEN THE HENS are done, remove them from the grill and serve warm with the sauce. ◉

Grilled Cornish Hens Oriental with Glass Noodles

Fritz Sonnenschmidt

½ cup soy sauce

2 teaspoons crushed garlic plus 1 large clove, crushed

2 tablespoons five spice powder

½ teaspoon ground black pepper plus more to taste

2 tablespoons sesame oil

4 Cornish hens, split, with breastbone and wings removed

2 teaspoons green peppercorns

½ cup red wine

½ cup brown sauce, homemade or store-bought

½ cup heavy cream

Salt to taste

Glass noodles, cooked according to package directions

1 tablespoon butter

4 sprigs cilantro, grilled, for garnish

IN A SMALL BOWL, combine the soy sauce, 2 teaspoons garlic, five spice powder, ½ teaspoon black pepper, and sesame oil and blend well. Pour over the Cornish hens in a casserole dish and marinate for 2 to 3 hours in the refrigerator.

REMOVE THE HENS from the marinade and grill them over medium heat for 8 minutes on each side.

IN A SKILLET over medium-high heat, dry-roast the green peppercorns for 2 to 3 minutes. Add the red wine and crushed garlic clove and reduce by half. Add the brown sauce and cream, season with salt and pepper, and bring to a boil. Lower the heat and simmer for 5 to 10 minutes. Strain the sauce with a fine-mesh sieve.

TO SERVE, toss the glass noodles in butter and divide among 4 plates. Top with a Cornish hen and surround with the sauce. Garnish with grilled cilantro sprigs. ◉

Glass noodles, also called slippery noodles, cellophane noodles, or Chinese vermicelli, are super-thin and translucent when dried. Made from the starch of mung beans, they have a wonderful glassy and slippery texture when cooked.

SERVES 4

Grilled Duck with Mango Chutney Sauce

Fritz Sonnenschmidt

This recipe proves not only how easy brining is but how sensational the results are. When making the brine, remember to plan carefully and do as much as possible in advance.

SERVES 4

4 quarts water plus 6 cups ice water

2 cups kosher salt

2 cups brown sugar

1 onion, quartered

1 orange, quartered

6 whole star anise seeds

10 cloves garlic, crushed

½ cup sliced fresh ginger

¼ cup soy sauce

3 tablespoons pickling spice

2 (6-pound) ducks, split in half

Olive oil

Mango Chutney Sauce

1 tablespoon olive oil

1½ cups chopped red onion

6 cloves garlic, thinly sliced

3 ripe mangos, peeled, pitted, and coarsely chopped

4 cups chicken stock

1 cup honey

5 tablespoons balsamic vinegar

1 tablespoon minced fresh ginger

½ cup chopped parsley

Salt and pepper to taste

White rice, cooked

IN A LARGE STOCKPOT, combine 4 quarts water, the salt, brown sugar, onion, orange, anise, crushed garlic, ginger, soy sauce, and pickling spice and bring to a boil. Remove the pot from the heat, add 6 cups ice water, and cool. Add the split ducks and marinate in this brine for 6 to 8 hours.

REMOVE THE DUCKS from the brine and pat dry with paper towels. Spray with olive oil. Grill the ducks over high heat on both sides. Reduce the grill heat to medium, place the ducks in a roasting pan, and grill for approximately 30 to 40 minutes more. Remove the ducks from the grill and allow to rest for 5 minutes.

IN A CASSEROLE over medium–high heat, heat the olive oil. Add the onions and garlic and sauté for 5 minutes. Add the mangos and sauté for 4 minutes more. Add the chicken stock, honey, vinegar, and ginger and simmer, stirring occasionally, until a thick sauce forms, for 1 to 1½ hours. Remove the sauce form the heat, add the parsley, and season with salt and pepper.

REMOVE THE BREASTBONE from the ducks and serve with chutney sauce and cooked rice. ◉

Grilled Chicken Thai Style

Fritz Sonnenschmidt

More and more people are discovering the wonderful, bold flavors of Thai food, like the ones in this dish. Turmeric, with its brilliant yellow color, is closely related to ginger and often used in Thai and Indian cooking.

SERVES 4

2 tablespoons powdered lemongrass

1 teaspoon ground turmeric

1 teaspoon garlic powder

Salt and pepper to taste

2 whole chickens, split, with backbones removed

Olive oil to spray plus 4 tablespoons

12 ounces romaine or iceberg lettuce or long green beans

6 tablespoons sake

¼ cup sugar

10 tablespoons rice vinegar

2 tablespoons Thai fish sauce (nam pla)

2 cloves garlic, roasted

1½ teaspoons chili sauce

2 tablespoons chopped cilantro

White rice, cooked

IN A SMALL BOWL, combine the lemongrass, turmeric, garlic powder, salt, and pepper. Rub this mixture into the chicken. Spray with oil and grill over medium–high heat, turning every 5 minutes until done, 20 to 30 minutes.

WASH THE LETTUCE well and dry. In a medium bowl, blend the sake, sugar, rice vinegar, fish sauce, garlic, chili sauce, cilantro, and 4 tablespoons olive oil. Add the lettuce and marinate for 30 minutes.

GRILL THE LETTUCE over medium–high heat for 1 minute on each side, up to 6 minutes. Remove to a serving plate and spoon some of the marinade on top.

REMOVE THE CHICKEN from the grill and remove the breastbones. Place on top of the lettuce. Serve with rice. ◉

Seafood

Grilled Salmon with Balsamic Butter Sauce and Apple Fennel Salad

Fritz Sonnenschmidt

½ cup butter

3 tablespoons balsamic vinegar

1 tablespoon honey

1 tablespoon golden mustard

Salt and pepper to taste

4 (7-ounce) salmon steaks

Olive oil

Apple Fennel Salad

1 cup apple cider or juice

6 tablespoons olive oil

¼ cup vinegar

2 teaspoons honey

Salt and pepper to taste

11 Granny Smith apples, cut into wedges

1 medium fennel bulb, trimmed and cut into wedges

10 ounces arugula, trimmed and washed

½ cup crystallized pecans (nuts cooked in simple syrup until liquid evaporates, then coated with a little oil to prevent sticking), for garnish

HEAT THE BUTTER in a skillet until golden in color. Add the vinegar, honey, mustard, salt, and pepper. Brush salmon steaks with this sauce and spray with olive oil. Grill the salmon over medium–high heat, approximately 4 minutes on each side. Remove from the grill and keep warm.

TO MAKE THE SALAD, combine the cider, olive oil, vinegar, and honey. Season with salt and pepper and mix well. Add the apples, fennel, and arugula and toss.

GRILL THE APPLES and fennel over high heat for 2 minutes on each side. Place the arugula on the grill for 1 minute each side, then season with salt and pepper.

PLACE ARUGULA on individual plates and top with the apples and fennel. Place the salmon on the salad. Garnish with crystallized pecans and serve. ◉

The only way to keep fish from sticking to the grill is to use an ample amount of oil, most of which will burn off during the cooking process. Salmon steaks, which usually have some skin left on, are a sturdy fish to grill and don't fall apart very easily.

SERVES 4

Black tiger shrimp, widely farmed in Asia, are readily available in the United States. They are distinguished by their black stripes and large size.

SERVES 4

Grilled Tiger Shrimp with Curried Arborio Rice Cakes, Black Olives, and Fire-Roasted Red Pepper Sauce

Marcel Desaulniers

1 tablespoon extra virgin olive oil

½ cup finely minced onion

Salt and freshly ground black pepper to taste

1 tablespoon curry powder

1 cup arborio rice

½ cup dry white wine

2¾ cups well-seasoned chicken stock

2 large red bell peppers, washed

1 teaspoon balsamic vinegar

1 pound tiger shrimp, peeled and deveined

½ pound spinach, trimmed, washed, and dried

24 black olives, pits removed

HEAT THE OLIVE OIL in a medium saucepan over medium heat. When hot, add the onions, season with salt and pepper, and cook, stirring frequently, until the onions are tender, about 2 minutes. Add the curry powder, stir to combine, and cook for 1 minute more. Add the rice and stir to combine. Add the white wine and cook, constantly stirring, until the wine is absorbed, about 2 minutes. Add 1 cup of hot chicken stock and continue to cook, constantly stirring the rice until the stock is absorbed, about 4 minutes. Add 1 more cup of chicken stock and cook, once again constantly stirring, until the stock is absorbed, about 6 minutes. Add ½ cup of hot chicken stock and cook, stirring constantly, until the rice is thick and creamy, about 5 minutes. Season with salt and pepper (be certain to taste the rice mixture and adjust the seasoning as needed). Pour the rice mixture out onto a 10 by 15-inch nonstick baking sheet with sides and spread the mixture over half of the sheet (the thickness of the mixture will prevent it from running over onto the other half after it is spread out), to a uniform thickness. Refrigerate the rice mixture, uncovered, until thoroughly chilled, about 1 to 1½ hours.

PLACE THE PEPPERS on the grill over high heat and char, turning frequently, until the skin is uniformly blackened and blistered, about 10 minutes. Remove the peppers from the grill and rinse the charred skin off the peppers under cold running water. Remove and discard the skins, stems, seeds, and the inner membranes, leaving the roasted red pepper flesh. Transfer the roasted pepper flesh to a small saucepan with the remaining ¼ cup chicken stock and the balsamic vinegar. Over high heat, bring to a boil. Remove the pot from the heat. Use an emersion blender or a food processor fitted with a metal blade to purée this mixture. Season with salt and pepper and keep warm.

REMOVE THE RICE CAKE from the refrigerator. Turn the baking sheet over onto a clean, dry cutting board, lifting the baking sheet off the rice mixture. Cut the solidified rice cake into 16 equal rectangles. Place the cakes, evenly spaced, onto a clean, dry nonstick baking sheet and place the baking sheet on a side of the grill not directly over the heat. Roast the rice cakes until slightly crispy outside but deliciously moist and tender inside, about 20 to 25 minutes.

DIVIDE THE SHRIMP into 4 portions and thread them onto skewers. Season with salt and pepper. Grill the shrimp over a medium fire for 1½ minutes to 2 minutes on each side; be careful not to overcook, as the shrimp can go from tender to tough in a matter of seconds.

PLACE A GENEROUS pile of spinach in the center of a large serving plate Arrange the warm rice cakes around the spinach. Dress the greens with the pepper sauce. Sprinkle the olives over the greens. Place the shrimp on the greens and serve immediately. ◉

Grilled Shrimp with Fresh Cucumber and Kimchi Salad

Chris Schlesinger | Reprinted from *Salsas, Sambals, Chutneys & Chow Chows*, Quill Press

3 unpeeled cucumbers, cut into thirds, then finger-sized pieces

1 carrot, peeled and cut into finger-sized pieces

1 red bell pepper, cut into thin strips

½ cup salt

1 bunch watercress, well washed and trimmed of stems

1 tablespoon minced garlic

1 tablespoon minced fresh ginger

2 tablespoons sugar

¼ cup white vinegar

3 tablespoons paprika

1 tablespoon minced red or green chile pepper

2 tablespoons sesame seeds, toasted in 350° oven for 5 minutes

1 teaspoon crushed white pepper

16 medium shrimp

2 tablespoons oil

Salt and pepper

RUB CUCUMBERS, carrots, and bell pepper strips all over with the salt. Place in a large bowl, cover with plastic wrap, and refrigerate for 2 hours. Rinse very well and drain.

ADD watercress, garlic, ginger, sugar, vinegar, paprika, chile pepper, sesame seeds, and white pepper to the salted vegetables and mix well. Refrigerate.

MEANWHILE, brush the shrimp with the oil and season with salt and pepper. Grill over medium–high heat for 3 to 4 minutes per side. To check for doneness, cut into one shrimp and see that it is opaque all the way through.

ON A SERVING PLATTER, place the grilled shrimp over a bed of kimchi. Serve immediately. ◉

You'll find *kimchi* on nearly every Korean table in different variations, but it always starts with vegetables that have been soaked in salted water for several hours. Store-bought varieties usually have a good deal of heat in them, something you can control when you make it yourself.

SERVES 2 AS AN ENTREE AND 4 AS AN APPETIZER

Grilled Lobster Tails with Spicy Cucumber-Watermelon Relish

Chris Schlesinger | Relish recipe reprinted from *Salsas, Sambals, Chutneys & Chow Chows*, Quill Press

Spicy Cucumber-Watermelon Relish

2 unpeeled cucumbers, washed, halved, and thinly sliced

1 cup watermelon chunks the size of playing dice, seeded

½ small red onion, thinly sliced

1 carrot, peeled and thinly sliced

¼ cup rice wine vinegar or white vinegar

¼ cup sugar

1 teaspoon crushed red pepper flakes

1 tablespoon chopped fresh mint

1 tablespoon chopped cilantro

Salt and freshly cracked white pepper to taste

4 to 6 (6- to 8-ounce) lobster tails

Salt and pepper

IN A LARGE BOWL, combine all the relish ingredients. Mix well and set aside. (This relish will keep, covered and refrigerated, for 4 to 5 days.)

SEASON THE LOBSTER tails with salt and pepper and place, flesh side down, on a well-oiled grill. Grill the lobster tails over medium heat for 8 to 10 minutes or until done. The exposed meat should be opaque.

SERVE THE LOBSTER tails immediately with the relish on the side. ◉

This relish is a variation of the classic cucumber relishes so common in Southeast Asia. The addition of watermelon makes it truly special. It goes well with any grilled shellfish.

SERVES 4 TO 6

Mustard-Grilled Halibut Fillet with a White Bean, Carrot, and Watercress Salad

Marcel Desaulniers

¼ cup whole-grain mustard

2 tablespoons dry white wine

1 tablespoon cracked black peppercorns

1 teaspoon freshly squeezed lemon juice

¼ teaspoon salt

4 (6-ounce) halibut fillets

White Bean, Carrot, and Watercress Salad

1½ cups dry navy beans, picked over and soaked for 8 to 12 hours

5 tablespoons extra virgin olive oil

2 carrots (about ½ pound), peeled, ends removed, and cut into ¼-inch dice

Salt and white pepper to taste

½ cup fresh orange juice

1 tablespoon sherry wine vinegar

1 tablespoon fresh chopped celery leaves

1 bunch watercress (about ½ pound), leaves only, washed, and dried

COMBINE THE MUSTARD, white wine, cracked peppercorns, lemon juice, and salt in a medium bowl. Whisk to combine. Place the halibut fillets in the marinade and thoroughly coat. Cover the bowl with plastic wrap and refrigerate for 30 minutes to 1 hour.

DRAIN THE SOAKED BEANS into a colander. Rinse the beans with cold water, and drain thoroughly. Place the beans in a large stockpot and cover with 3 quarts cold water. Over high heat, bring the water to a boil. Reduce the heat, and simmer until the beans are tender, about 30 minutes. Drain the water from the beans, transfer them to a medium bowl, and set aside.

Halibut is a firm, fine-textured fish that grills well, especially if you buy it as a steak with the skin still on. Watercress, with its refreshingly pungent and peppery taste, is an excellent accompaniment to the halibut's white, delicate meat.

SERVES 4

WHILE THE BEANS are cooking, heat 2 tablespoons olive oil in a medium sauté pan over medium–high heat. Add the diced carrots, season with salt and pepper, and sauté stirring frequently until half cooked, about 12 minutes. Add the orange juice and simmer until the carrots are tender and the orange juice has almost completely evaporated, about 5 minutes. Transfer the carrots to the bowl of white beans and combine. Add the remaining 3 tablespoons olive oil, sherry wine vinegar, and chopped celery leaves. Season with salt and white pepper and stir to combine. Set aside while grilling the fish.

REMOVE THE FISH from the marinade. Grill the fish over medium heat for about 4 to 5 minutes per side. For more well-cooked fish, place on the top rack of the grill for an additional 2 to 3 minutes per side.

ADD THE WATERCRESS leaves to the white bean and carrot mixture and toss to combine. Place an equal amount of salad in the center of each plate. Top each salad with a halibut fillet and serve immediately. ◉

Grilled Rainbow Trout with Grilled Fingerling Potatoes, Tiny Green Beans, Herbed Black Olives, and Tomatoes

Marcel Desaulniers

3 pounds fingerling potatoes

¼ cup extra virgin olive oil

Salt and pepper to taste

1 pound tiny green beans, ends trimmed

32 black olives, pits removed

3 tomatoes, skins and seeds removed, cut into ¼-inch dice

3 tablespoons balsamic vinegar

¼ teaspoon chopped fresh parsley

¼ teaspoon chopped fresh tarragon

¼ teaspoon chopped fresh thyme

¼ teaspoon chopped fresh oregano

4 whole rainbow trout, about 10 ounces each

3 tablespoons salad oil

1 teaspoon lemon juice

PLACE THE POTATOES in a large stockpot and cover with cold water. Bring to a boil over high heat. Reduce the heat and simmer until the potatoes are tender, about 45 minutes. Drain the potatoes and cool them thoroughly under cold running water. Pat dry with paper towels. Cut the potatoes in half lengthwise and transfer to a medium bowl. Add 2 tablespoons olive oil, season with salt and pepper, and toss to combine. Set aside.

BRING 3 QUARTS of salted water to a boil in a 5-quart pot over medium-high heat. Add the green beans and cook until tender, about 4 to 6 minutes depending on the thickness of the bean. Drain the beans, then immediately plunge into ice water to stop the cooking and keep the beans bright green. Drain again thoroughly.

Fingerling potatoes may cost more than other varieties, but their silky texture and creamy richness make them worth the indulgence. Transplanted from France, they have only been grown in the United States for the last five years.

SERVES 4

COMBINE THE BEANS, olives, and tomatoes in a medium bowl. Add the remaining 2 tablespoons olive oil, balsamic vinegar, and the chopped fresh herbs. Season with salt and pepper and stir to combine. Hold at room temperature while grilling the potatoes and the trout.

GRILL THE POTATOES over medium heat for about 3 to 4 minutes on each side or until well marked. Transfer the potatoes to the upper rack of the grill to finish cooking while you grill the fish.

REMOVE THE HEADS, tails, and belly fins from the whole trout. Rinse the fish very well under cold running water and pat dry with paper towels. Combine the salad oil and lemon juice in small bowl and whisk together. Drizzle this lemon oil over the trout. Season the trout with salt and pepper and grill over medium-high heat for about 4 minutes on each side (depending on the thickness of your trout).

EVENLY DIVIDE the salad among 4 plates. Place an equal amount of the grilled potatoes around the outside of the salads. Place a grilled fish on the top of each salad and serve immediately. ◉

Grilled Tea Shrimp with Sweet and Sour Sauce

Fritz Sonnenschmidt

16 large shrimp, peeled and deveined

1 teaspoon finely ground tea

Juice of 1 lemon

¼ cup olive oil

1 onion, diced

¼ cup minced ginger

1 cup sweet pickle relish

2 cups tomato juice

2 tablespoons honey

2 tablespoons vinegar

1 tablespoon soy sauce

1 to 2 tablespoons cornstarch

Salt and ground pepper to taste

White rice, cooked

IN A LARGE BOWL, combine the shrimp with the tea, lemon juice, and 1 table-spoon olive oil. Toss and marinate for 30 minutes.

THREAD THE SHRIMP onto skewers for easy grilling. Grill the shrimp over medium heat for 3 minutes on each side. Remove from the grill and keep warm.

IN A MEDIUM SAUCEPAN, heat the remaining 3 tablespoons olive oil over medium-high heat. Add the onion and ginger and sauté for 2 minutes. Add the pickle relish, tomato juice, honey, vinegar, and soy sauce and bring to a boil. Mix the cornstarch with a little water and stir into the sauce to thicken it slightly. Season with salt and pepper.

REMOVE THE SHRIMP from the skewers and serve with the sauce and rice. ◉

Here's another secret ingredient from Maestro Fritz—tea! Used as a rub on the shrimp, it adds great flavor and color. Be careful not to overcook the shrimp or they will become rubbery.

SERVES 4

Charred-Raw Yellowfin Tuna with Snow Peas and Curried Fire-Roasted Yellow Pepper Sauce

Marcel Desaulniers

1 (2 by 2 by 12-inch) fresh yellowfin tuna loin

½ cup salad oil

Salt and freshly cracked black pepper

Fire-Roasted Yellow Pepper Sauce

1 tablespoon extra virgin olive oil

¼ cup finely diced yellow onion

Salt and white pepper to taste

1 tablespoon curry powder plus extra for garnish

¼ cup dry white wine

1 cup fresh chicken stock

2 large yellow bell peppers (about 1 pound), fire roasted, skinned, seeded, and cut into 1-inch pieces

¼ teaspoon finely chopped fresh thyme leaves

¼ teaspoon finely chopped fresh oregano leaves

2 ounces frisée, washed and cut into approximately 1-inch pieces

½ pound fresh snow peas, ends trimmed, blanched in boiling salted water, and shocked in ice water

1 large tomato, peeled, seeded, and cut into ¼-inch pieces

1 tablespoon freshly cracked black pepper

continued on next page

Highly esteemed yellowfin tuna has a rose-colored flesh and is prized by sushi chefs.

SERVES 4

Charred-Raw Yellowfin Tuna with Snow Peas and Curried Fire-Roasted Yellow Pepper Sauce (continued)

COAT THE TUNA LOIN with ¼ of the salad oil. Season the loin with the salt and black pepper. Char the loin on an extremely hot grill on all sides for 4 minutes (1 minute each side). Baste the loin with the remaining oil as it chars (this will create a torrent of flame to help char the tuna loin). Transfer the tuna loin from the grill to a large dinner plate and place in the freezer for 15 minutes to stop the cooking. Remove the charred loin from the freezer and cut into 4 equal pieces. Refrigerate until needed.

HEAT THE OLIVE OIL in a medium saucepan over medium heat. Add the onions, season with salt and white pepper, and sauté until tender, about 2 minutes. Add the curry powder and white wine and continue to cook for 2 more minutes. Add the chicken stock and roasted peppers and bring to a boil. Reduce the heat and simmer until most of the liquid has evaporated, about 5 to 7 minutes. Transfer the roasted pepper mixture to the bowl of a food processor fitted with a metal blade. Liquefy the pepper mixture until smooth. Strain the sauce. Add the chopped thyme and oregano. Season with salt and white pepper, and chill in an ice-water bath until cold. Refrigerate the cold sauce until needed.

EVENLY DIVIDE the roasted pepper sauce among 4 plates. Place a small bed of frisée in the center of the sauce and place the tuna loin on the greens. Artfully arrange the snow peas and the tomatoes around the plate and in the sauce. Finally, garnish the plates with the cracked black pepper and curry powder. Serve immediately or hold in the refrigerator for up to 30 minutes. ◉

Grilled Catfish with Coriander Black Beans in a Saffron Lemon Vinaigrette

Fritz Sonnenschmidt

Coriander Black Beans

½ pound dried black beans

1½ teaspoons baking soda

3 slices bacon

2 tablespoons chopped red onions

6 cloves garlic, minced

¾ teaspoon dried basil

¾ teaspoon ground cumin

2 tablespoons coriander seeds, crushed

3 cups light beer

1 teaspoon salt

Saffron Lemon Vinaigrette

¼ cup freshly squeezed lemon juice

Grated zest of 1 lemon

2 tablespoons finely chopped red onion

2 pinches saffron (10 strings)

1 teaspoon honey

½ cup olive oil

Salt and freshly ground black pepper to taste

¼ cup olive oil

1 to 2 tablespoons lemon juice

2 large cloves garlic, minced

1 tablespoon chopped chives

4 (7-ounce) catfish fillets

2 Japanese eggplants, cut into rounds ½ inch thick

1 red bell pepper, cut in half and stems and seeds removed

continued on next page

There's nothing boring about beans cooked in beer and coriander, and they make a delightful accompaniment to the catfish. Try to get thick pieces of catfish that will hold up well on the grill.

SERVES 4

Grilled Catfish with Coriander Black Beans in a Saffron Lemon Vinaigrette (continued)

RINSE THE BLACK BEANS, place in a plastic bucket, and cover with water. Fold in the baking soda and leave overnight.

DRAIN AND RINSE the beans well. In a skillet over medium–high heat, sauté the bacon. Add the onions and garlic and sauté for 3 minutes. Add basil, cumin, and coriander seeds and sauté for 3 more minutes. Add the black beans. Add beer to cover the beans. Simmer for 1 to 1½ hours until tender. Add salt.

TO MAKE THE VINAIGRETTE, blend the lemon juice, zest, onion, and saffron together and allow to rest for 1 hour. Fold in the honey and allow to rest for another 15 minutes. Whisk in the oil slowly, then season with salt and pepper.

FOR THE CATFISH, combine the olive oil, lemon juice, garlic, and chives. Pour this marinade over the catfish, sliced eggplants, and red pepper. Marinate for 20 minutes.

GRILL THE CATFISH over medium–high heat for 3 to 4 minutes on each side or to desired doneness. Grill the eggplant slices and the red peppers for 1 to 2 minutes on each side. Slice the pepper for serving.

PLACE THE BLACK BEANS on a serving platter, top with the catfish, surround with the eggplant and red pepper, and drizzle the vinaigrette over the fish and eggplant. ◉

Grilled Loin of Monkfish with Wax Bean Succotash

Marcel Desaulniers

Monkfish, a longtime favorite in Europe and Asia, has also become popular in the United States over the last ten years. The mild-flavored fish holds up well in grilling.

SERVES 4

¾ pound yellow wax beans, trimmed

4 large ears fresh sweet corn, husk and silk removed

2 tablespoons unsalted butter

1 onion (about 6 ounces), peeled and cut into ¼-inch pieces

1 large red bell pepper, washed, cored, seeded, membrane removed, and cut into ¼-inch pieces

1 large green bell pepper, washed, cored, seeded, membrane removed, and cut into ¼-inch pieces

Salt and freshly cracked black pepper to taste

1 cup heavy cream

1 large tomato, peeled, seeded, and cut into ¼-inch pieces

1 teaspoon chopped fresh parsley

1 teaspoon chopped fresh thyme

1½ pounds fresh monkfish loin, well trimmed

2 teaspoons fresh lemon juice

IN A STOCKPOT, bring 3 quarts well-salted water to a boil over high heat. Blanch the wax beans in the boiling water for 6 minutes, until tender. Transfer the beans to a bowl of ice water to stop the cooking. Set aside. Blanch the corn in the same pot of boiling water for about 10 minutes, until the kernels are tender. Transfer the corn to a bowl of ice water to stop the cooking. Cut the kernels from the cobs. Set the corn aside.

HEAT THE BUTTER in a large sauté pan over medium-high heat. Add the onion and bell peppers, season with salt and pepper, and sauté for 2 minutes. Add the corn and the wax beans and toss to combine. Add the heavy cream and stir. Reduce the heat and simmer until thick, about 6 minutes. Add the chopped tomato, parsley, and thyme. Stir to combine and keep warm.

SEASON THE MONKFISH with the lemon juice, salt, and pepper. Grill the loins over medium heat for 4 minutes on each side, until nicely charred and cooked. Divide the succotash among 4 plates. Slice the monkfish loins into ½-inch-thick bias-cut pieces and place on top of the succotash. Serve immediately. ◉

Curried Salmon with Squash, Tomatoes, and Grilled Scallion Vinaigrette

Marcel Desaulniers

16 scallions, washed and roots and tops trimmed

¼ cup balsamic vinegar

1 tablespoon fresh lemon juice

2 teaspoons Dijon mustard

¾ cup safflower oil

Salt and freshly cracked black pepper to taste

¼ cup extra virgin olive oil

1 large zucchini (about 1 pound), washed and sliced on the bias into ½-inch-thick pieces

1 large yellow squash (about 1 pound), washed and sliced on the bias into ½-inch-thick pieces

4 (6-ounce) salmon fillets, skin and pin bones removed

2 teaspoons curry powder

4 medium tomatoes (about 1½ pounds), washed, cored, and sliced ¼ inch thick

GRILL THE SCALLIONS over a hot fire for about 2 minutes on each side, until well marked. Transfer them to a cutting board and chop 8 of the grilled scallions into ⅛-inch pieces, reserving the remaining 8 for garnish. Set aside.

IN A MEDIUM BOWL, whisk together the balsamic vinegar, lemon juice, and mustard. Add the safflower oil in a slow, steady stream while whisking, until incorporated. Season with salt and pepper and whisk to combine. Add the chopped scallions to the vinaigrette and stir to combine. Cover with plastic wrap and set aside.

LIGHTLY BRUSH the olive oil onto the zucchini and yellow squash slices. Season with salt and pepper. Grill over a hot fire for about 3 minutes on each side. Remove from the grill and keep warm.

LIGHTLY DUST the salmon fillets with the curry powder. Season with salt and pepper. Grill the salmon over a medium–hot fire for 3 to 4 minutes on each side.

ARTFULLY ARRANGE the tomato slices and grilled squashes on the plates. Dress the vegetables with the vinaigrette. Place the grilled fish on top and garnish with the remaining grilled scallions. Serve immediately. ◉

Curry powders can differ greatly in taste and levels of heat, so be sure to experiment until you find one you like. Madras curry powders are hotter than the standard blends.

SERVES 4

Meat

Beef Tenderloin with Sparkler Radishes, Dandelion Greens, and Szechuan Peppercorn Vinaigrette

Marcel Desaulniers

4 tablespoons cider vinegar

3 tablespoons fresh lemon juice

2 teaspoons freshly cracked Szechuan peppercorns

¾ cup extra virgin olive oil

Salt and white pepper to taste

1½ pounds trimmed beef tenderloin, cut into 1-inch cubes

¼ pound dandelion greens, stemmed, washed, and dried

1½ pounds sparkler radishes, ends trimmed, and washed thoroughly

IN A MEDIUM BOWL, whisk together the cider vinegar, lemon juice, and Szechuan peppercorns. Add the olive oil in a slow, steady stream while whisking to incorporate. Season with salt and pepper. Cover with plastic wrap and set aside.

THREAD THE BEEF cubes onto skewers and season with salt and pepper. Grill over a medium-high heat for 4 to 5 minutes for medium-rare, longer for more well-done. Keep warm.

PLACE THE GREENS in the center of a serving plate. Lightly dress the greens with the vinaigrette. Toss the radishes in some of the vinaigrette and place on the greens. Remove the skewers from the beef and arrange the meat around the plate. Serve immediately. ◉

Dandelion greens, a traditional component of salads in the South, are best eaten before the plants flower or they can become bitter. Sparkler radishes are hard to find, but worth the search. They are round, bright red with a distinctive white tip, juicy and sweet with a mild peppery finish.

SERVES 4

Apple Cider—Marinated Grilled Pork Tenderloin with Maple-Scented Sweet Potatoes and Grilled Red Onions

Marcel Desaulniers

3 cups fresh apple cider

2 tablespoons light brown sugar

½ teaspoon ground cinnamon

¼ teaspoon fresh ground nutmeg

1 pound well-trimmed pork tenderloin, cut into 16 medallions, ¼ inch thick

Salt and pepper

4 large sweet potatoes, skin removed, cut into quarters and held in cold water

4 tablespoons unsalted butter

¼ cup pure maple syrup

1 large red onion, peeled and cut into ½-inch-thick slices

1 tablespoon salad oil

COMBINE THE CIDER, brown sugar, cinnamon, and nutmeg in a medium plastic container. Stir to dissolve the sugar and spices. Season the pork tenderloin with salt and pepper. Add the pork to the apple cider mixture and marinate at least 30 minutes.

PLACE THE SWEET POTATOES in a medium saucepan and fill with fresh cold water to cover. Over high heat, bring to a boil. Reduce the heat and simmer until the potatoes are tender, about 18 minutes. Strain the potatoes and return them to the pan. Add the butter and the maple syrup. Mash the sweet potatoes until they are smooth and the butter and maple syrup are thoroughly incorporated. Cover the pan with plastic wrap and keep warm.

continued on next page

This dish was choreographed with some wonderful sweet and smoky flavors that come together into a dazzling finish. Be sure not to overcook the pork or it will dry out.

SERVES 4

Apple Cider—Marinated Grilled Pork Tenderloin with Maple—Scented Sweet Potatoes and Grilled Red Onions (continued)

BRUSH THE ONION slices with the oil and season generously with salt and pepper. Grill the onion slices over a medium–hot fire until nicely charred and cooked through, about 3 minutes on each side. Keep the onions warm while grilling the pork.

SEASON THE PORK MEDALLIONS with salt and black pepper. Quickly grill the medallions over a medium–hot fire on both sides, being sure not to overcook, for about 1½ to 2 minutes.

EVENLY DIVIDE the sweet potatoes among 4 plates. Break apart the grilled onion rings and artfully arrange them on the plates. Top each plate with the grilled pork and serve. (Feel free to garnish the dishes with a touch of fresh chopped herbs. My favorite is rosemary.) ◉

Grilled Skewer of Smoked Lamb with Spaghetti Squash and Mint Pesto

Marcel Desaulniers

1½ cups warm water

¾ cup clover honey

2 tablespoons kosher salt

1 cup crushed ice cubes

1½ pounds well-trimmed lamb meat, cut into 1-inch pieces

1 large spaghetti squash (about 4 pounds)

Salt and black pepper to taste

4 ounces fresh mint leaves

½ cup toasted walnut pieces

¼ cup olive oil

20 cherry tomatoes, washed, cut in half, and slow roasted

Smokers are relatively inexpensive and a great way to slow-cook barbecued meats. Here the lamb is placed in a brine, then cold-smoked at a temperature of 100° before it is finished on the grill.

SERVES 4

COMBINE THE WARM WATER, ½ cup honey, and the kosher salt in a medium bowl. Whisk to dissolve. Add the crushed ice and stir until it has melted and the liquid is cold. Add the lamb and stir to combine. Allow the lamb to soak for 2 to 3 minutes in the brine. Remove the meat from the brine and divide it evenly on 4 skewers. Place the lamb skewers in your smoker, and cold-smoke for 45 to 50 minutes. Transfer the lamb skewers to the refrigerator.

PREHEAT THE OVEN to 250°F.

WHILE THE LAMB is smoking, cut the spaghetti squash in half lengthwise and remove the seeds. Rub the inner cavities with the remaining honey. Season with salt and pepper. Transfer the squash halves to a medium roasting pan. Fill the bottom of the pan with about ½ inch of water. Place the pan on one side of a hot grill (the side not directly over the heat) and roast until the squash is almost tender, about 1 hour and 15 minutes. Remove the squash from the grill. Scoop out the flesh onto a dinner plate and set aside.

COMBINE THE MINT LEAVES and walnuts in a small food processor fitted with a metal blade. Process the mint and nuts for 15 seconds on high. Slowly add the oil and continue to chop for 10 more seconds. Scrape down the bowl and chop for a final 10 seconds. Set aside.

SEASON THE LAMB SKEWERS with salt and pepper. Grill the lamb over a medium-high heat for 3 minutes on each side. While the lamb is grilling, heat the roasted spaghetti squash, slow-roasted tomatoes, and mint pesto in a hot sauté pan over medium heat. Adjust the seasoning. Place an equal amount of the pesto-scented squash and tomatoes on the center of each plate. Place the smoked grilled lamb on the top, remove the skewers, and serve immediately. ◉

Szechuan peppercorns with their tiny seeds may look like black peppercorns but are quite different. They have a distinctive flavor that is accentuated by toasting.

SERVES 4

Garlic and Soy–Marinated Flank Steak with Brown Butter, Broccoli, and Mashed Red Bliss Potatoes

Marcel Desaulniers

1 tablespoon Szechuan peppercorns

¼ cup soy sauce

1 tablespoon sugar

1 tablespoon chopped garlic

½ cup vegetable oil

4 (6- to 8-ounce) flank steaks

2 pounds Red Bliss potatoes, quartered and covered with cool water

12 tablespoons (¾ cup) unsalted butter

2 tablespoons sour cream

Salt and white pepper to taste

1 medium bunch broccoli (about 1 pound), trimmed into florets

TOAST THE PEPPERCORNS in a pie tin on the grill for 3 minutes. Cool them to room temperature before roughly cracking them. In a medium bowl, whisk together the soy sauce and sugar until the sugar has dissolved. Add the garlic and stir to incorporate. Add the vegetable oil in a slow, steady stream, while whisking, until emulsified and thick. Add the cracked peppercorns and whisk to combine. Add the flank steak and turn a few times to coat with the marinade. Cover the bowl with plastic wrap and refrigerate for at least 2 hours (and up to 24 hours).

RINSE THE POTATOES a few times with cold running water. Place them in a medium-sized saucepan and cover with cool water. Bring to a boil over high heat. Reduce the heat and simmer until the potatoes are very tender but not mushy, about 30 minutes. Drain and mash the potatoes, return them to the pan and place over low heat. Stir the potatoes with a wire whisk for 4 minutes, allowing any excess moisture to evaporate. Add 6 tablespoons butter and 2 tablespoons sour cream. Stir with a wire whisk to combine. Season the potatoes with salt and white pepper, cover, and keep warm until needed.

GRILL THE FLANK STEAKS over a medium-hot fire for 3 minutes on each side for rare. (For medium, transfer the flank steak to the upper rack in your grill and continue to cook for 10 minutes.) Remove the meat from the grill and allow it to rest while you prepare the broccoli.

BRING 2 QUARTS lightly salted water to a boil in a large saucepan over medium-high heat. Cook the broccoli in the water until tender, 3 minutes. Drain thoroughly in a colander. Heat the remaining 6 tablespoons butter in a very hot sauté pan until lightly browned. Add the broccoli, season with salt and pepper, and cook over medium heat until warmed through, about 3 to 4 minutes.

DIVIDE THE POTATOES and mound in the center of each plate. Surround with the broccoli. Slice the steak into thin slices across the grain and place on each mound of potatoes. Serve immediately. ◉

Grilled Pork Loin Medallions with Country Ham and Pecan–Studded Jasmine Rice

Marcel Desaulniers

Try to get a top-quality ham for this dish. Many top-quality ham producers in the South are now providing their products through mail order.

SERVES 4

2 tablespoons unsalted butter

½ cup minced yellow onion

Salt and white pepper to taste

1 cup jasmine rice

1¾ cups chicken stock, heated

Freshly ground black pepper to taste

1½ pounds Lean Generation pork tenderloin, trimmed of fat and silver skin, cut into 1½-ounce pieces and lightly pounded ¼ inch thick

4 (⅛-inch-thick) slices country ham

1 cup toasted pecan halves

½ pound fresh watercress, trimmed, washed, and dried

1 tablespoon each finely diced carrot, red bell pepper, yellow squash, and zucchini

HEAT THE BUTTER in a medium saucepan over medium–high heat. Add the yellow onion, season with salt and white pepper, and sauté for 2 minutes, until tender. Add the rice and stir to coat with the butter and onions. Add the hot chicken stock and stir to blend. Bring to a boil. Cover, reduce the heat to medium, and continue to cook until the rice is tender, about 15 minutes. Remove from the heat and season with salt and black pepper. Keep warm.

SEASON THE PORK medallions with salt and black pepper. Quickly grill them over medium–high heat on both sides, being sure not to overcook, for 1½ to 2 minutes.

EVENLY DIVIDE the jasmine rice among 4 plates. Fashion a cone out of the sliced country ham and place it in the center of the rice facing up. Fill these "cornucopias" with some of the watercress. Place 4 pieces of the grilled pork on top of the rice on each plate. Stud the rice with the toasted pecans and sprinkle each plate with some of the diced vegetables. Serve immediately. ◉

Pepper-Crusted Grilled Strip Loin Steak with Homemade Steak Sauce and Mushroom Hobo Packs

Chris Schlesinger | Reprinted from *How to Cook Meat*, HarperCollins Publishers

Three different regions— New York, Texas, and Kansas City—all lay claim to the strip loin steak, an extremely tender cut of beef. It has many other names as well, including ambassador steak or club steak. Whatever you call it, it's a great steak for the grill.

SERVES 4 TO 6

Steak Sauce

2 tablespoons olive oil

1 medium onion, peeled and thinly sliced

1 cup shrimp shells, 1 teaspoon chopped anchovies, or
*   1 teaspoon chopped sardines (optional)*

1 tablespoon minced garlic

1 tablespoon minced fresh ginger

1 tablespoon minced fresh chile peppers

1 cup white vinegar

1 cup beer

1 cup pineapple juice

½ cup molasses

3 tablespoons tomato paste

5 whole chives

1 tablespoon ground cumin

2 tablespoons freshly cracked black pepper

1 shot Scotch, rye, or bourbon

¼ cup soy sauce

1 lime, very thinly sliced

Hobo Packs

2 pounds mushrooms (any kind), trimmed

⅓ cup extra virgin olive oil

2 tablespoons minced garlic

¼ cup roughly chopped fresh herbs, such as sage, thyme, and/or oregano

2 tablespoons dry sherry

Kosher salt and freshly cracked black pepper to taste

continued on page 102

Pepper–Crusted Grilled Strip Loin Steak with Homemade Steak Sauce and Mushroom Hobo Packs (continued)

4 (12- to 16-ounce) strip loin steaks, about 1½ inches thick

1 cup freshly cracked black pepper

Kosher salt

IN A LARGE SAUCEPAN, heat the oil over medium–high heat until hot but not smoking. Add the onion and cook, stirring occasionally, until golden brown, 11 to 13 minutes. Add the shrimp shells, garlic, ginger, and chiles. Cook, stirring occasionally, for 2 minutes. Add the remaining sauce ingredients and bring to a boil. Reduce the heat and simmer for 2 hours, stirring occasionally. Strain the sauce, pushing the solids with a wooden spoon to extract all the liquid. The sauce should have about the same consistency as standard Worcestershire sauce. Set aside.

SHOVE ABOUT three–quarters of the coals to one side of the grill for a hot fire and about one-quarter to the other side for a medium–hot fire.

TEAR OFF 8 SHEETS of heavy–duty foil, each about 2 feet long, and stack them one on top of the other. Arrange half the mushrooms in the center of the top sheet and drizzle with half of the olive oil. Sprinkle half the minced garlic, half the herbs, and half the sherry over the mushrooms and season with salt and pepper. Fold up the top 4 sheets of foil around the vegetables, one after the other, turning the package one quarter turn between each sheet and making sure each sheet is well sealed. Repeat this process with the remaining ingredients so that you have 2 packs. Place the packs on the bottom of the grill off to one side, pile coals up around them, and cook for about 30 minutes, depending on the intensity of the coals.

MEANWHILE, PAT THE STEAKS dry with paper towels and season with the pepper and a generous amount of salt. Place them on the grill over the hot fire and cook until well seared, 4 to 5 minutes per side. Move to the medium–hot fire and continue to cook to desired doneness, 10 to 12 minutes more for rare. To check for doneness, make a ¼–inch cut in the thickest part of the meat; it should be slightly less done than you like it. Remove the steaks from the heat, cover loosely with foil, and let rest for 5 minutes.

UNWRAP THE HOBO PACKS and serve with the steaks, passing the steak sauce on the side. ◉

Grilled Veal T-Bones with a Hobo Pack of Fig, Prosciutto, and Spinach

Chris Schlesinger | Reprinted from *How to Cook Meat*, HarperCollins Publishers

2 cups trimmed, well-washed, and dried spinach

4 ounces thinly sliced prosciutto

6 fresh figs, halved

1 large tomato (about the size of a baseball), cored and diced

1 tablespoon minced garlic

⅓ cup extra virgin olive oil

15 fresh sage leaves

Kosher salt and freshly cracked black pepper to taste

4 (12-ounce) veal loin chops, about 1½ inches thick

3 tablespoons cracked coriander seeds, or 1 teaspoon ground coriander

TO MAKE THE HOBO PACK, tear off 4 sheets of heavy-duty foil, each about 2 feet long, and stack them one on top of the other. In a large bowl, combine the spinach, prosciutto, figs, tomato, garlic, olive oil, sage, salt, and pepper and toss well to combine. Place this mixture in the center of the top sheet of foil, then fold up the sheets of foil around the ingredients, one after the other, turning the package one quarter turn between each sheet and making sure each sheet is well sealed.

IN A MEDIUM-HOT GRILL, place the hobo pack on the outside periphery of the coals, where the fire is less intense. Pile the coals around them and cook for about 20 minutes.

MEANWHILE, DRY THE VEAL chops with paper towels, sprinkle them generously with salt and pepper, and coat them well with the coriander, pressing gently so it adheres. Grill the chops until well seared on one side, 5 to 7 minutes. Turn and continue cooking to the desired doneness, 5 to 7 minutes more for medium-rare. To check for doneness, make a ¼-inch cut in the thickest part of the meat; it should be slightly less done than you like it.

ALLOW THE CHOPS to rest for about 5 minutes while you open the hobo pack and divide the contents among four plates. Top each plate with a veal chop and serve. ◉

This Italian-inspired dish combines figs, sage, and prosciutto, which are cooked in a hobo pack. Pork loin chops work well as a substitute for the veal.

SERVES 4

Southeast Asian–Style Grilled Skirt Steak with Aromatic Greens and Ginger–Lime Dressing

Chris Schlesinger | Reprinted from *How to Cook Meat*, HarperCollins Publishers

Skirt steak has become a favorite among grillers because of its rich flavor and reasonable cost. It needs to be cooked quickly over high heat and cut very thinly on the bias for serving or it will be tough.

SERVES 4

¼ cup soy sauce

2 tablespoons cracked coriander seeds, or 1 tablespoon ground coriander

2 tablespoons freshly cracked white pepper, or 1 tablespoon ground white pepper

1½ pounds skirt steak, cut into 4 portions

Ginger–Lime Dressing

¼ cup olive oil

2 tablespoons Asian sesame oil

1 teaspoon sugar

¼ cup fresh lime juice (from about 4 limes)

2 tablespoons minced fresh ginger

1 to 3 teaspoons finely minced fresh chile peppers

Kosher salt and freshly cracked black pepper to taste

2 bunches arugula, trimmed, washed, and dried

1 cup fresh mint leaves

1 cup cilantro leaves (some stems are okay)

1 cup fresh Thai basil leaves or regular basil

1 large carrot, peeled and cut into matchsticks

1 red bell pepper, cored, seeded, and cut into matchsticks

1 cucumber, peeled, seeded, and cut into matchsticks

½ cup unsalted peanuts, toasted and chopped, for garnish

IN A SHALLOW DISH, combine the soy sauce, coriander, and white pepper and mix well. Place the steaks in the dish and turn to coat well.

GRILL THE STEAKS over high heat until well seared on one side, about 4 minutes. Turn and continue to cook to desired doneness, about 6 minutes total cooking time for rare. To check for doneness, make a ¼-inch cut in the thickest part of the meat; it should be slightly less done than you like it. Remove the steaks from the grill, cover loosely with foil, and allow to rest while you make the dressing.

IN A MEDIUM BOWL, whisk the dressing ingredients together until well combined. Place the arugula, herbs, carrot, bell pepper, and cucumber in a large bowl. Add as much dressing as you like and toss well.

THINLY SLICE THE STEAK on the bias, against the grain. Place a serving of greens on each plate, top with a few slices of steak, and garnish with the peanuts. ◉

Crusty Grilled Butterflied Leg of Lamb with Smoky Eggplant–Fig Relish

Chris Schlesinger | Reprinted from *How to Cook Meat*, HarperCollins Publishers

Ask your butcher to bone, trim, and flatten the lamb leg so its thickness is as uniform as possible. The meat should be pinkish red, since the darker the color, the older the lamb.

SERVES 6 TO 8

3 tablespoons cumin seeds, or 1½ tablespoons ground cumin

3 tablespoons coriander seeds, or 1½ tablespoons ground coriander

¼ cup black peppercorns, or 2 tablespoons freshly cracked black pepper

¼ cup dried oregano, crumbled

3 tablespoons kosher salt

1 (4- to 5-pound) boned and butterflied leg of lamb, 2 to 2½ inches thick

10 large garlic cloves, peeled and halved lengthwise

¼ cup olive oil

Smoky Eggplant–Fig Relish

2 cups dry red wine, such as pinot noir

2 tablespoons sugar

2 tablespoons honey

½ cinnamon stick, or 1 teaspoon ground cinnamon

Minced zest of ½ lemon (yellow part only; about 2 tablespoons)

8 ounces dried figs, quartered (about 1½ cups)

1 large eggplant, cut into ½-inch slices

1 large onion, peeled and quartered

3 tablespoons olive oil

1 tablespoon finely minced garlic

Kosher salt and freshly cracked black pepper to taste

¼ cup fresh lemon juice (from about 1 lemon)

¼ cup roughly chopped fresh parsley

continued on page 108

Crusty Grilled Butterflied Leg of Lamb with Smoky Eggplant–Fig Relish (continued)

IF USING WHOLE SPICES, put the cumin, coriander, and peppercorns in a small heavy sauté pan and toast over medium heat, shaking the pan frequently, until the spices are fragrant, 2 to 3 minutes. Cool, then coarsely grind the spices in a coffee grinder, spice grinder, or mortar and pestle. Stir in the oregano and salt and set aside. (If using ground spices, combine and mix well.)

MAKE 20 SMALL SLITS in the surface of the lamb and push a piece of garlic into each one. Rub the lamb with oil, then rub it all over with the spice mixture, pressing lightly to be sure it adheres.

SHOVE ABOUT three-quarters of the coals to one side of the grill for a hot fire and about one-quarter to the other side for a medium fire. Place the lamb directly over the hot fire, fat side up, and sear well, about 10 minutes. Turn and sear the second side, about 10 minutes more. Move to the medium-hot side and grill, turning once, for 5 to 10 minutes more, until the meat is done to your liking. Check for doneness with a meat thermometer: 120°F is rare, 126°F is medium-rare (which is how we like it), 134°F is medium, 150°F is medium-well, and 160°F is well-done. Otherwise check for doneness by making a ¼-inch cut in the thickest part of the meat; it should be slightly less done than you like it. Remove the lamb from the grill, cover loosely with foil, and let rest for 10 to 20 minutes.

MEANWHILE, MAKE THE RELISH. In a small saucepan, combine the wine, sugar, honey, cinnamon, lemon zest, and figs. Stir and bring just to a simmer over medium-high heat. Reduce the heat and simmer gently for 12 minutes. Remove from the heat, remove and discard the cinnamon stick, and set aside.

RUB THE EGGPLANT SLICES and onion quarters with the olive oil and season with the garlic, salt, and pepper. Grill the vegetables over medium-high heat until they are well browned and the eggplant slices are moist all the way through, 5 to 6 minutes per side. Let cool slightly, then chop the vegetables and add them to the fig sauce. Add the lemon juice and parsley, stir well to combine, and season with salt and pepper.

CUT THE LAMB into thin slices against the grain and serve with the relish. ◉

Molasses-Glazed Pork Tenderloin with Seared Sweet-and Sour Red Onions and Sage-Date Power Pack

Chris Schlesinger | Adapted from *How to Cook Meat*, HarperCollins Publishers

3 tablespoons olive oil

2 red onions, peeled and thinly sliced

3 (12- to 14-ounce) pork tenderloins, trimmed of external fat

Kosher salt and freshly cracked black pepper

⅓ cup molasses

¼ cup dry red wine

3 tablespoons balsamic vinegar

⅓ cup chopped pitted dates

¼ cup roughly chopped fresh sage

1 teaspoon minced garlic

2 tablespoons extra virgin olive oil

Pork tenderloin (not to be confused with pork loin) is not only the tenderest cut of pork, but its fat content is similar to a boneless, skinless chicken breast. It's important to sear it well, allowing it to really brown.

SERVES 4 TO 5

PREHEAT THE OVEN to 450°F.

IN A LARGE OVENPROOF sauté pan, heat 2 tablespoons of the oil over medium-high heat until hot but not smoking. Add the onions and cook, stirring occasionally, until golden brown, 11 to 13 minutes. Remove the onions to a bowl.

DRY THE TENDERLOINS with paper towels and sprinkle them generously with salt and pepper. Add the remaining 1 tablespoon oil to the pan and heat until the oil is hot but not smoking. (Note: If your pan is not large enough to comfortably hold the 3 tenderloins, use 2 smaller pans.) Add the tenderloins and sear well on all sides, about 12 minutes total.

COMBINE THE MOLASSES and wine in a small bowl. Grill the tenderloins over medium-high heat, brushing them generously with the molasses mixture after about 8 minutes, until they are done to your liking (10 to 14 minutes for medium-well). Check for doneness with a meat thermometer: It should read 150°F. Or check by making a ¼-inch cut in the thickest part of the meat; it should look slightly less done than you like it. Remove the pork from the grill, brush once more with the molasses mixture, cover loosely with foil, and let rest for 10 minutes.

ADD THE BALSAMIC VINEGAR to the onions and toss to combine thoroughly. In a small bowl, combine the dates, sage, garlic, and olive oil and mix well. Carve the pork into slices about 1 inch thick. Place the onions on individual serving plates, top with the sliced pork, and sprinkle with the date mixture. ◉

Unlike most rib recipes, this "EZ" one has you precook the ribs in a low oven before taking them outside to the grill. This is especially convenient if you want to make them a day ahead or if hungry friends can't wait for the ribs to cook. The results are still succulent and wonderful.

SERVES 5

EZ-Style Adobo Pork Ribs with Molasses-Chile Barbecue Sauce

Chris Schlesinger | Reprinted from *How to Cook Meat*, HarperCollins Publishers

Flavoring Paste

2 tablespoons minced garlic

2 tablespoons ground cumin

2 tablespoons chile powder

2 tablespoons dark brown sugar

3 tablespoons kosher salt

3 tablespoons freshly cracked black pepper

¼ cup roughly chopped fresh oregano

¼ cup rough chopped cilantro

6 tablespoons orange juice

2 tablespoons fresh lime juice (from about 1 lime)

4 dashes Tabasco sauce

2 tablespoons olive oil

2 (3-pound) racks pork spareribs

Molasses-Chile Barbecue Sauce

⅓ cup molasses

½ cup ketchup

¼ cup fresh lime juice (from about 2 limes)

2 tablespoons ground cumin

½ cup roughly chopped cilantro

1 to 3 tablespoons minced fresh chile peppers

PREHEAT THE OVEN to 200°F.

IN A FOOD PROCESSOR or blender, combine the paste ingredients and blend until smooth. Dry the ribs with paper towels, then rub them thoroughly with the paste. Place the ribs on two baking sheets and slow-roast for 3 hours, until red juice comes out when you poke the meat with a fork. The meat will be tender and pull easily from the bone. Remove the ribs from the oven. They can go right onto the grill, stand out for a while, or be refrigerated, covered, for up to 2 days.

WHILE THE RIBS are roasting, combine the sauce ingredients in a small bowl and mix well. Set aside.

GRILL THE RIBS on a high rack set over low heat and let them stay there as long as your patience allows. A light crust on the outside is the goal, and depending on your fire, it can be achieved in 5 minutes per side or take up to 30 minutes per side, if you're into prolonging your guests' agony. Of course, the longer the ribs cook, the better. Brush them with the sauce during the last minute on the grill.

CUT THE RIBS apart between the bones and serve the remaining barbecue sauce on the side. ◉

Grilled Lamb Chops with Grilled Romaine Lettuce and Shepherd's Potatoes

Fritz Sonnenschmidt

It's become increasingly popular to grill romaine lettuce as people discover the great results in both taste and texture. Ask your butcher for the double-cut lamb chops, which make a dramatic presentation.

SERVES 6

2 tablespoons grated fresh ginger

1 cup light soy sauce

¼ cup dry white wine

2 heaping tablespoons brown sugar

3 tablespoons toasted sesame oil

3 heads romaine lettuce, trimmed, washed, and cut in half lengthwise

Olive oil for spraying plus ½ cup

3 tablespoons kosher salt

1½ tablespoons ground black pepper

2½ tablespoons dried fresh marjoram

1½ tablespoons garlic powder

6 (⅓- to ½-pound) double lamb chops

3 pounds russet potatoes

4 tablespoons fresh lemon juice

2 tablespoons finely chopped shallots

1 tablespoon chopped fresh parsley

2 cloves grilled garlic, mashed

IN A BLENDER, combine the ginger, soy sauce, white wine, brown sugar, and sesame oil, and process until well blended. Brush the romaine halves with the marinade, then spray with olive oil. Grill over medium heat for 2 to 3 min– utes. Turn the romaine halves, brush again with the marinade, and grill for 3 to 4 more minutes. Remove the romaine from the grill and keep warm.

IN A SMALL BOWL, combine the salt, pepper, 1½ tablespoons of the marjoram, and the garlic powder and mix well. Rub into the lamb chops. Spray the chops with olive oil. Grill approximately 3 to 4 minutes on each side or to desired doneness. Keep warm.

IN A LARGE STOCKPOT filled with salted water, boil the potatoes until fork tender. Drain the potatoes and place in the refrigerator to chill. When chilled, cut potatoes into wedges lengthwise. In a large bowl, combine the ½ cup olive oil, lemon juice, shallots, remaining 1 tablespoon marjoram, parsley, mashed garlic, and the potato wedges and toss. Marinate for 30 minutes.

GRILL THE POTATOES over medium heat for 5 to 10 minutes, turning 2 or 3 times during grilling.

ARRANGE THE LAMB CHOPS and potatoes on individual plates. Serve with the grilled romaine. ◉

Grilled Veal Chops with Red Wine Cranberry Sauce

Fritz Sonnenschmidt

1 teaspoon salt

1 teaspoon blackberry tea

½ teaspoon black pepper

4 (7 ounce) veal chops

2 tablespoons olive oil

4 scallions, washed and trimmed

Red Wine Cranberry Sauce

4 tablespoons (¼ cup) soft butter

2 large shallots, finely diced

1 cup red wine

6 crushed black peppercorns

1 cup brown sauce (homemade or store-bought)

1 tablespoon sugar

2 ounces fresh cranberries

Salt and pepper to taste

Riced potatoes

IN A SMALL BOWL, combine the salt, tea, and pepper. Rub this seasoning into the veal chops and brush with olive oil. Grill the chops over medium–high heat for 6 to 7 minutes each side. Grill the scallions for 1 to 2 minutes.

TO MAKE THE SAUCE, heat 2 tablespoons of the butter in a skillet over medium–high heat. Add the shallots and sweat for 2 minutes. Add the red wine and peppercorns, bring to a boil, and reduce by half. Add the brown sauce and sugar and cook for 3 to 5 minutes. Strain the sauce and return it to the skillet. Add the cranberries and cook for 3 to 4 minutes more. Fold in the remaining 2 tablespoons butter and season with salt and pepper.

SERVE THE VEAL CHOPS with the sauce and riced potatoes, garnished with the grilled scallions. ◉

Maestro Fritz recommends that this dish be served with riced potatoes. To make, put boiled potatoes through a potato ricer, a gadget that can be purchased at any gourmet store. Many chefs prefer the texture of riced potatoes over mashed.

SERVES 4

Grilled Pork Chops with White Bean Ragout and Sundried Tomato Sauce

Fritz Sonnenschmidt

Here's an upscale menu for outdoor cooking, even though *ragout* is just the French word for stew.

SERVES 4

1 heaping cup white beans

5 cups chicken stock

¼ cup olive oil

½ cup chopped red onion

½ cup finely chopped carrots

½ cup finely chopped celery

5 teaspoons finely chopped fresh thyme, or 2 teaspoons dried thyme

1 tablespoon grated orange zest

Salt and pepper to taste

4 (8-ounce) pork chops, approximately 1 inch thick

Sundried Tomato Sauce

1 cup sundried tomatoes

1 cup white wine

¼ cup vinegar

½ teaspoon ground black pepper

1 bay leaf

1 tablespoon olive oil

1 cup chicken stock

½ cup heavy cream

1 tablespoon chopped fresh thyme

Salt and sugar to taste

RINSE THE WHITE BEANS and combine with the chicken stock in a large pot. Bring to a boil and simmer, covered, for about 1 hour or until tender. Drain, saving ¾ cup of the cooking liquid.

HEAT 3 TABLESPOONS of the oil over medium–high heat in a heavy skillet. Add the onions, carrots, and celery and sauté for 5 minutes. Add the thyme and the orange zest. Add the beans and the reserved cooking liquid and simmer for 10 minutes. Season with salt and pepper.

SEASON THE PORK CHOPS with salt and pepper. Brush the chops with the remaining oil and grill over medium-high heat for 3 minutes per side or to desired doneness.

TO MAKE THE SAUCE, bring sundried tomatoes, white wine, and vinegar to a boil in a small saucepan. Add the pepper and bay leaf and cook to reduce to about 4 tablespoons, 10 minutes. Remove the bay leaf, add the olive oil, and purée with a handheld blender. Add the chicken stock, cream, and thyme and simmer for 5 minutes. Season with salt and sugar.

TO SERVE, spoon the bean ragout on each plate. Top with a pork chop and spoon the tomato sauce over the chops. ◉

Grilled Corned Beef and Cabbage with Balsamic Vinaigrette

Fritz Sonnenschmidt

This dish gives you the flexibility of cooking some things indoors the day ahead and others out on the grill.

SERVES 6

1 orange

10 whole cloves

1 (4-pound) beef brisket, rinsed well

2 tablespoons caraway seeds

10 cloves garlic

1 bay leaf

3 pounds Yukon Gold potatoes

1 head savoy cabbage, cut in 6 wedges

2 pounds small carrots, cut in half lengthwise

Salt and pepper to taste

Olive oil to spray plus ¼ cup

6 parsley sprigs

Assorted mustards

Balsamic Vinaigrette

1½ cup olive oil

½ cup balsamic vinegar

Salt and pepper to taste

1 tablespoon chopped parsley or chives

½ teaspoon golden mustard (optional)

¼ teaspoon sugar or to taste

STUD THE ORANGE with the cloves. Place the beef in a large stockpot with the orange, 4 teaspoons of the caraway seeds, garlic, and bay leaf. Cover with water, bring to a boil, and simmer for 3 hours, uncovered. Remove the beef and allow to cool.

ADD THE POTATOES to the cooking liquid and boil until fork tender. Remove and allow to cool.

SEASON THE CABBAGE and the carrots with salt and pepper and spray with oil. Cut the potatoes in half and toss with the remaining 2 teaspoons caraway seeds and ¼ cup oil.

CUT THE BEEF into 1-inch-thick slices.

GRILL THE CABBAGE over medium-high heat for 3 minutes per side, turning twice, for 15 minutes. Grill the carrots for 2 minutes per side, turning twice, for 8 minutes. Grill the potatoes for 2 minutes each side. Grill the beef slices for 2 minutes per side, turning twice, for 8 minutes. Add the parsley sprigs and grill 1 minute.

COMBINE ALL the vinaigrette ingredients and blend well.

ARRANGE THE BEEF, cabbage, carrots, and potatoes on a serving platter and garnish with the parsley. Serve with the vinaigrette and extra mustard, if desired. ◉

Grilled Pork Tenderloin Asian Style with Grilled Rice Cakes

Fritz Sonnenschmidt

Rice cakes are a wonderful side dish for the grill, as most of the work is done the day ahead. After they are grilled, the cakes should have a crusty, crisp outside and a soft, creamy inside.

SERVES 4

2 (1-pound) pork tenderloins, cut into 3-ounce medallions (about 3 inches thick pounded to 1½ inches thick)

Tea, salt, and freshly ground black pepper

Arrowroot for dusting plus 4 teaspoons arrowroot or cornstarch

2 tablespoons peanut oil

1 to 2 tablespoons olive oil

1 large poblano chile, seeded and cut into matchsticks

1 red bell pepper, seeded and cut into matchsticks

6 scallions, white part only, chopped

1 tablespoon balsamic vinegar

2 tablespoons soy sauce

2½ cups chicken stock

1 tablespoon oyster sauce

3 cloves garlic, roasted and mashed

½ cup green seedless grapes, cut in half

Pinch of sugar

1 cup rice

PREHEAT THE OVEN to 400°F.

SEASON THE PORK MEDALLIONS with tea, salt, and pepper. Dust with arrowroot and brush heavily with peanut oil. Grill the pork over medium heat for 2 minutes on each side or to desired doneness.

HEAT THE OLIVE OIL in a skillet, add the chile and red pepper, and sweat for 2 minutes. Add the scallions, vinegar, soy sauce, ½ cup chicken stock, oyster sauce, roasted garlic, and grapes. Bring to a boil and thicken with 4 teaspoons arrowroot. Season with ground pepper and sugar.

IN AN OVENPROOF SAUCEPAN, combine the rice, the remaining 2 cups chicken stock, and salt and pepper to taste and bring to a boil. Cover and cook in the oven for 20 minutes. Line a baking sheet with parchment paper and spray with oil. Spread the rice mixture 1 inch thick and place in the refrigerator to chill. Cut the rice into rectangles, brush with oil, and grill over medium heat for 2 minutes each side.

SERVE PORK MEDALLIONS with the pepper and grape sauce and the rice cakes. ◉

Grilled Sirloin Steak with Grilled Caraway Potatoes and Grilled Oysters

Fritz Sonnenschmidt

2 tablespoons freshly ground coffee

1 tablespoon salt plus more to taste

4 (7-ounce) sirloin steaks

Olive oil to spray plus 2 tablespoons

4 medium russet potatoes, boiled, peeled, and cut in half lengthwise

1 teaspoon caraway seeds

Pepper to taste

8 oysters on the half shell

8 tablespoons cocktail sauce

IN A SMALL BOWL, combine the coffee and 1 tablespoon salt and rub into the steaks. Spray the steaks with olive oil and grill over medium heat for 5 minutes on each side or to desired doneness.

PLACE THE POTATOES in a large bowl and add the caraway seeds, 2 tablespoons olive oil, salt, and pepper. Toss to coat and grill the potatoes over medium heat.

TOP THE OYSTERS with cocktail sauce and spray with a little oil. Grill over medium heat for 5 to 8 minutes.

REMOVE STEAKS, potatoes, and oysters to individual plates and serve ●

Be sure to buy oysters that are still alive—look for ones with tightly closed lids. They can be stored in the refrigerator for approximately 3 days. Remember not to overcook or they will toughen.

SERVES 4

Index

Permissions

From *How to Cook Meat* by Chris Schlesinger and John Willoughby (HarperCollins, 2000) © 2000 by Chris Schlesinger and John Willoughby: Pepper-Crusted Black and Blue Steak and Spicy Sesame Spinach with Soy-Wasabi Dipping Sauce; Pepper-Crusted Grilled Strip Loin Steak with Homemade Steak Sauce and Mushroom Hobo Packs; Southeast Asian-Style Grilled Skirt Steak with Aromatic Greens and Ginger Lime Dressing; Grilled Veal T-Bones with a Hobo Pack of Fig, Prosciutto, and Spinach; Crusty Grilled Butterflied Leg of Lamb with Smoky Eggplant-Fig Relish; EZ-Style Adobo Pork Ribs with Molasses-Chile Barbecue Sauce; Molasses-Glazed Pork Tenderloin with Seared Sweet-and-Sour Red Onions and Sage-Date Power Pack.

From *License to Grill* by Chris Schlesinger and John Willoughby (William Morrow and Company, 1997) © 1997 by Chris Schlesinger and John Willoughby: Grilled Shrimp and Bacon Skewers; Corn Bread-Stuffed Barbecued Game Hens; Grilled and Chilled Mediterranean-Style Gazpacho; Grilled Sesame Chicken Skewers.

From *Lettuce in Your Kitchen* by Chris Schlesinger and John Willoughby (William Morrow and Company, 1996) © 1996 by Chris Schlesinger and John Willoughby: Tommy's Red Cabbage Salad with Grilled Pineapple; Arugula and Duck Salad with Mango, Carmelized Onions, and Spiced Pecans; Dr. Hibachi's Spinach Salad with Grilled Lamb; Arugula and Radicchio with Grilled Mozzarella and Bread Skewers.

From *Salsa, Sambals, Chutneys & ChowChows: Intensely Flavored "Little Dishes" from around the World* by Chris Schlesinger and John Willoughby (Quill Press, 1995) © 1997 by Chris Schlesinger and John Willoughby: Grilled Shrimp with Fresh Cucumber and Kimchi Salad; Spicy Cucumber-Watermelon Relish.

From *The Thrill of the Grill: Techniques, Recipes & Down-Home Barbecue* by Chris Schlesinger and John Willoughby (William Morrow and Company, 1990) © 1990 by Chris Schlesinger and John Willoughby: Grilled West Indies Spice-Rubbed Chicken Breast with Grilled Banana.

The following recipes are courtesy of Marcel Desaulniers: Grilled Asparagus and Sautéed Wild Mushrooms on Toasted Brioche; Grilled Pound Cake and Sweet Peach Napoleon with Crystal Cream; A Panoply of Grilled Mushrooms, Asparagus, and Artichokes in a Rosemary-Scented Grilled Tomato Broth; Grilled Skewers of Ginger Chicken with Fennel and Sweet Bell Peppers; Pepper-Charred Boneless Quail with Crisp Apple Slaw and Warm Smoked Bacon Dressing; Herb-Grilled Chicken Breast with Pineapple Basmati Rice and Pink Grapefruit Butter; Grilled Turkey Scaloppine with Fire-Roasted Corn, Grilled Tomatoes, and Spinach Cream; Curried Salmon with Squash, Tomatoes, and Grilled Scallion Vinaigrette; Grilled Tiger Shrimp with Curried Arborio Rice Cakes, Black Olives, and Fire-Roasted Red Pepper Sauce; Mustard-Grilled Halibut Fillet with a White Bean, Carrot, and Watercress Salad; Grilled Rainbow Trout with Grilled Fingerling Potatoes, Tiny Green Beans, Herbed Black Olives, and Tomatoes; Charred-Raw Yellowfin Tuna with Snow Peas and Curried Fire-Roasted Yellow Pepper Sauce; Grilled Loin of Monkfish with a Wax Bean Succotash; Apple Cider-Marinated Grilled Pork Tenderloin with Maple-Scented Sweet Potatoes and Grilled Red Onions; Garlic and Soy-Marinated Flank Steak with Brown Butter, Broccoli, and Mashed Red Bliss Potatoes; Beef Tenderloin with Sparkler Radishes, Dandelion Greens, and Szechuan Peppercorn Vinaigrette; Grilled Pork Loin Medallions with Country Ham and Pecan-Studded Jasmine Rice; Grilled Skewer of Smoked Lamb with Spaghetti Squash and Mint Pesto.

The following recipes are courtesy of Fritz Sonnenschmidt: Chicken Wings Teriyaki; Chicken Wings Americana, Chicken Wings Asian Style, Chicken Wings Ming Style; Grilled Vegetarian Club Sandwich; Mexican Shrimp Cocktail; Pecan and Brown Sugar Crescents with Grilled Peaches in Blue Cheese Cabernet Sauvignon; Fresh Fruit from the Grill; Country Corn and Scallop Luncheon Salad; Grilled Vegetable Medley with Blue Cheese Butter; Grilled Asparagus Salad with Grilled Swiss Cheese and Prosciutto; Vegetarian Lentil Pie; Grilled Duck with Mango Chutney Sauce; Grilled Chicken Thai Style; Grilled Cornish Hens Oriental with Glass Noodles; Grilled Tea Shrimp with Sweet and Sour Sauce; Grilled Catfish with Coriander Black Beans in a Saffron Lemon Vinaigrette; Grilled Salmon with Balsamic Butter Sauce and Apple Fennel Salad; Grilled Lamb Chops with Grilled Romaine Lettuce and Shepherd's Potatoes; Grilled Veal Chops with Red Wine Cranberry Sauce; Grilled Pork Tenderloin Asian Style with Grilled Rice Cakes; Grilled Sirloin Steak with Grilled Caraway Potatoes and Grilled Oysters; Grilled Pork Chops with White Bean Ragout and Sundried Tomato Sauce; Grilled Corned Beef and Cabbage with Balsamic Vinaigrette.

Acknowledgments

We'd like to salute our three grilling maestros, Marcel Desaulniers, Chris Schlesinger, and Fritz Sonnenschmidt, C.M.C., who created the wonderful recipes you find in this book. We often refer to them as the "dream team," a title they earned with their unwavering professionalism, tremendous culinary talents, delightful humor, and endless cooperation. No matter how many hours we kept them in front of the camera filming the companion television series–whether rain or a hot sun beat down on them–they were a pure joy to work with.

Grilling Maestros would have never been possible without the incredible support of our sponsor, Beaulieu Vineyard, and the tireless and steadfast Priscilla Felton, who has been a true champion of the project. We are grateful both to her and her wonderful staff, Lynn Higgens and Robert Larsen, who helped us with this project on a daily basis, staying after hours, patiently and efficiently taking care of endless details. They graciously allowed us to use the beautiful grounds of Beaulieu Vineyard in the Napa Valley to tape the programs, never flinching when we moved in with truck after truck of equipment.

We are also very grateful to the Weber-Stephens Company who provided us with the grills used in the programs. We are especially indebted to Mike Kempster, Sr., who is a walking encyclopedia of grilling. He spent untold hours giving us advice and guidance, and graciously shared the tremendous knowledge and insights that Weber has gleaned from customers over the years. Mike's unwavering belief that everyone can be a successful backyard cook has been a great inspiration to the project.

Another great supporter of the project is Cuisinart, a company that truly devotes itself to great cooking. We deeply appreciate the support from Paul Ackels (a yet-to-be–discovered master of backyard cooking) and his belief that this program could be a serious tool for educating the public. Another special thank-you goes to our culinary devotee and supporter, Mary Rodgers, and her valuable assistance.

If you get a chance to watch the *Grilling Maestros* programs, you might wonder how the food miraculously appears on the set, always in the right quantity and always cooked to perfection. This was done through the tremendously hard work of our kitchen supervisor, Brett Bailey, along with Jason Wade. They both worked tirelessly and selflessly during long filming days to make sure that the execution of every recipe was flawless.

Finally, to all our viewers and purveyors of fine cuisine, we hope this book brings you many joyful hours of outdoor grilling.

The Producers: Marjorie Poore and Alec Fatalevich

Grilling Maestros 2 © 2001 by Marjorie Poore Productions
Photography by Alec Fatalevich
Design: Kari Perin, Perin+Perin
Editing: Barbara King
Production: Kristen Wurz

All rights reserved. No part of this book may be reproduced in any form
without written permission from the publisher.

ISBN 0-9651095-9-3
Printed in Singapore

10 9 8 7 6 5 4 3 2 1

MPP Books, 363 14th Avenue, San Francisco, CA 94118